26.2

MARATHON STORIES

26.2
MARATHON STORIES

KATHRINE SWITZER AND ROGER ROBINSON

RODALE

A RODALE/MADISON PRESS BOOK

Runner's WORLD

Runner's World® is a registered trademark of Rodale Inc.

Printed in Singapore

Cataloging-in-Publication data on file with the publisher

Distributed to the trade by Holtzbrinck Publishers

2 4 6 8 10 9 7 5 3 1 hardcover

Notice
Mention of specific companies, organizations, or authorities in this book
does not imply endorsement by the publisher, nor does mention of specific
companies, organizations, or authorities imply that they endorse this book.

Jacket credits: Front cover (clockwise from top left): Courtesy of Wellesley
College Archives; Panoramic Images/Getty Images; www.sporting-heroes.net;
D. Widmer; Edward Pond.
Back cover (clockwise from top left): Eadwaerd Muybridge; Boston Athletic
Association; Mariusz Peczek; IOC/Olympic Museum Collection; Enrico Lodi,
Maratona d'Italia Memorial Enzo Ferrari.

Produced for Rodale Inc. by

MADISON PRESS BOOKS
1000 Yonge Street, Suite 200
Toronto, Ontario, Canada
M4W 2K2
www.madisonpressbooks.com

Visit us on the Web at runnersworld.com, or call us toll-free at 800-848-4735

RODALE
LIVE YOUR WHOLE LIFE™

We inspire and enable people to improve their lives and the world around them
For more of our products visit **rodalestore.com** or call 800-848-4735

TO YOUNGSUN, WARREN, ANNE AND WAYNE SWITZER

CONTENTS

01

PRELUDE TO THE RACE

THE PRELUDE TO A MARATHON is one of life's strangest yet most vivid times. It is a time of intensity yet relaxation, apprehension yet resolve; a time of deeply introspective solitude in the midst of the biggest jostling throng most of us will ever join. So many people, intent on a separate inward commitment, but united in one common physical endeavor. Our motive is private, the context public. We are strangers who are instant comrades, competitors bonded by the shared knowledge that we are all about to undertake one of the hardest tasks in our lives. Ahead lie strenuous effort, weariness, and pain, but we will endure it all voluntarily, for the sheer enjoyment of trying.

The communal atmosphere before the start is tense, like an army awaiting the order to enter battle, because the marathon is a contest—and each runner will be tested. Yet the mood is also ebullient and exhilarating, like a troupe of actors before a performance, because the marathon is also a drama—and each runner's story will be part of the action.

The visible scene would surely baffle any unsuspecting Martian astronomer who happened to focus on it. Over a sprawling space of open ground wanders a huge swirling crowd of humans, of both genders and all races, ages, and sizes, nervous yet peaceful, who seem confined there yet are free to go; they are diverse and disorganized yet all wearing numbers, some grouped in teams but most alone; many with bare legs, covered in old shirts or plastic garbage bags to keep out the weather, yet who also wear expensive shoes and complex watches, milling about without direction; engaged in separate idiosyncratic rituals of shuffling and stretching, all lining up to enter—one by one—a row of wobbly little boxes; and somehow all coordinated and ready when the moment arrives to move together up to the start.

It seems a very strange business, but somehow it works. Once experienced, it is never forgotten.

Each marathon enhances the experience with its own pre-race setting: the trees and gracious wooden houses of Hopkinton, where the Boston Marathon begins, the Verrazano-Narrows Bridge soaring toward New York City, the swooping arc of the Sydney Harbour Bridge, the classical elegance of Greenwich Park beside the Thames, the fortress-like Pentagon, the high pillars of the Philadelphia Museum of Art, the broad ceremonial road to the Brandenburg Gate, the even grander beauty of the Champs-Elysées from the Arc de Triomphe, the

Previous spread: Runners fall quiet and still at the start of the Krakow Marathon, waiting for the gun, like dry wood about to flare into flame.

Right: The bus ride to the start seems to take forever, even for a champion like Paula Radcliffe, shown here heading toward her moment of truth in the ING New York City Marathon, 2004.

mountains towering over the starts at Pikes Peak and Taranaki, the Black Hills at Deadwood, the harbor at Victoria, the lakes at Siiver State, Kawaguchi, and Canberra, the river at Ottawa, the ocean at Big Sur, the world's longest urinal at Fort Wadsworth, at the start of the ING New York City Marathon, and many more.

Most marathons have their local pleasures and rituals: classical, jazz, country, or rock music; even the heroic, trembling, charismatic figure of Muhammad Ali, the familiar starter at Los Angeles; fireworks on festive Disney scale cascading out of the pre-dawn sky of Florida at the Walt Disney World Marathon; the line of horses that gallop with flashing hooves and fluttering manes in a nearly flying line alongside the runners at Napa Valley; the watchful giraffes and zebra at Safaricom in Kenya; or the sulfurous steam swirling around the runners from the hot cracked ground at Rotorua in New Zealand, where the very earth seems to take deep breaths before the start. Every marathon has its pre-start moment.

And the final moment before the race everywhere is the same, and it is magical. The music, the anthems, the speeches, the cheers, and the chatter all cease, and at last the runners are silent.

For runners, compulsively in motion, it is a unique moment of stillness. For 5 or 10 seconds everyone in that vast crowd looks silently inward and forward. All feel the premonitory glow, the flicker of readiness, like dry wood about to flare into flame. Then the gun is fired. And the marathon begins.

Left: Prelude to the drama. Nervous runners at the Flora London Marathon await the start of their 26.2 mile journey. Many wear disposable garbage bags against the rain.

Above: Dropping off the gear bag, in Krakow, Poland.

Right: So many rituals, so little time. As the clock ticks down, marathoners at the ING New York City Marathon mill around near the start. One runner takes a last-minute stretch.

02

THE STARTING LINE

THE STORY OF THE MARATHON began in 490 BC, with a runner and a battle. An invading army from Persia swept through northern Greece, and landed in the sheltered bay of Marathon, ready to attack the wealthy city-state of Athens, 25 miles away. The anxious Athenian generals dispatched a long-distance messenger to seek support from Sparta. His name was Pheidippides. Obviously a fit and resourceful "day runner," he covered the rocky, hilly 150 miles in about thirty hours, according to the Greek historian Herodotus. He then ran back with the disappointing answer that the Spartans would help only after the moon was full.

Pheidippides reported that during his homeward run, on Mount Parthenium, he had heard his name called out. It was the nature god Pan, who gave him another message—a complaint that the Athenians were negligent in worshiping him. We might attribute this story to the hallucination of an exhausted runner, but it impressed Herodotus. The incredible distance was not particularly noteworthy—running 300 miles was just the messenger's regular job.

As a running story, that's all there is. Herodotus tells how the outnumbered Athenians surprisingly won the Battle of Marathon, and marched quickly home in case the Persian fleet used another point of attack. He makes no mention of anyone running from Marathon to Athens (though no doubt several messengers did). Nor does he say anything about a runner dying from exhaustion while announcing the victory. That irresistible climax was added more than 500 years later, by Plutarch, a Greek writer in the Roman era. He mentions several collapsing messengers, including one from Marathon, "who ran in full armor, hot from the battle, and, bursting in at the doors of the first men of the State, could only say 'Hail! We are victorious!'" before expiring. The story had become colorful fiction.

The last leap into legend came in about 180 AD. The prose writer Lucian, discussing "Rejoice!" as a formal greeting (much like "Have a nice day"), mixed up the stories and named Pheidippides as the messenger from Marathon who died with the words "Rejoice! We are victorious!" The seed was planted.

It lay dormant for 1,700 years. Then in 1879 the English poet Robert Browning published a poem called "Pheidippides" in *Dramatic Idylls*, a book of verse stories. His version combines (and embellishes) the stories. His Pheidippides, inspired

Previous spread: Stone grooves mark the start for track races in Olympia, Greece, location of the original starting line and site of the most prestigious of the ancient Greek games.

Right: A late-19th-century engraving shows the messenger Pheidippides dying in heroic glory after delivering the joyous news of victory.

by love for "a maid," runs to Sparta and back, heroically insists on fighting in the battle, and asks the reward of carrying the news of victory. Browning's compelling verse captures the pace and energy of running. He also gives the runner the unforgettable words, "Rejoice, we conquer!"

All runners should read "Pheidippides." Michel Bréal, a French professor of languages, was so inspired by it that he wrote in 1894 to the planning committee for the revived Olympic Games in Athens proposing "a race from Marathon" with a prize to commemorate "the heroic messenger." The marathon footrace was born.

Dubious though the full story is historically, its appeal is eternal. Even if we remember Pheidippides only for running to Sparta and back (only!) he is a worthy runners' hero. He pushed beyond the limit, as every runner aspires to do.

The message from Marathon still inspires. How many thousands of marathon runners have thought as we cross the finish line, "Rejoice, we conquer!"

I ran and raced: like stubble, some field
which a fire runs through,
Was the space between city and city: two days,
two nights did I burn
Over the hills, under the dales, down pits
and up peaks…
He [Pan] was gone. If I ran hitherto—
Be sure that, the rest of my journey,
I ran no longer, but flew.
Parnes to Athens—earth no more,
the air was my road:
Here I am back. Praise Pan,
we stand no more on the razor's edge!…
He flung down his shield,
Ran like fire once more: and the space
'twixt the Fennel-field
And Athens was stubble again, a field
which a fire runs through,
Till in he broke: 'Rejoice, we conquer!'
Like wine through clay,
Joy in his blood bursting his heart,
he died—the bliss!

FROM "PHEIDIPPIDES," BY ROBERT BROWNING

Left: An ancient Greek vase depicts the economical fluency of distance runners.

Following spread: This Greek sarcophagus relief dating from 490 BC is one of many significant artworks showing the Battle of Marathon, the event that saved the Athens experiment of democracy.

03

OUT OF THE GATE

EVERYONE TALKS ABOUT the runner's mind in the final miles of a marathon—the struggle to survive, the will to push through pain, the determination to finish. But the first mile has its drama, too. It is the opening of the narrative that runs through the marathoner's head, the beginning of a story with an uncertain end.

When the gun fires, the first thought is that the moment has come at last. The runner thinks back to those long months of training that at times seemed unreal and never ending, to all the dark mornings and wet Sundays, the days of struggle and injury, the feelings of inadequacy when it seemed no progress was being made. The start brings a sense of finality and commitment. At that moment, the high-spirited exuberance of today's runners, cheering and whooping as they surge forward, strikes an exhilarating contrast to the loneliness and inwardness of so much of the training that has gone on before. Now it's really happening.

Exhilaration can be dangerous, however, when there are 25 more miles to run. Serious runners stay cool, avoiding the adrenaline rush, trying to enjoy the celebration yet remaining apart from it. (One experienced elite advises running as if inside a transparent bag, able to enjoy the festive experience but not becoming fully enveloped in it.) The start of all the big modern marathons is exciting enough: the jammed field slowly loosening, creating the freedom to run; the shuddering thunder of thousands of feet; the myriad people and outfits and running styles all around.

For years afterward, every runner can recall moments and incidents that make the first mile vivid in their race story. Many remember particular characters among the runners—the man with a loaf of bread on his head, the elegant blonde woman with twinkling jewelry, the squad of marines running in step, the foreign teams so purposeful in their matching uniforms. One frequent memory is of the small children along the sidelines who stretch out a hand and call, "Gimme five!" to the passing runners. (Some keep score of the hand slaps.)

There is also the shared experience, the indefinable energy that is generated when a large group of people focus on a common purpose—especially when motion is involved. As the first mile is completed, an unspoken unity can somehow be felt in the air. Then the "Mile 1" marker approaches. One down, 25 to go.

Previous spread: The wait is over at last, the crowd shuffles forward, and the race starts for real.

Right: The start at an early running of the famous *Le Cross du Figaro* in Paris.

Following spread: Runners cheerfully start a marathon in the scorching heat of the Sahara Desert.

04

OLYMPIC DISTANCE

GREECE WELCOMED THE IDEA of a race in the 1896 Olympics to commemorate the legend of Pheidippides. Greece was a poor country in the late 19th century, with few organized sports, so would have little chance in most events against practiced college athletes from other countries. The "marathon race" would demand only endurance and courage, which history had prepared the Greek people for only too well.

Hoping to inspire a local winner, Georgios Averoff, a generous financial supporter, added an antique vase to the silver marathon cup donated by Michel Bréal. There are stories that he also offered his daughter in marriage with a large cash dowry—but there are many unsubstantiated tales about this first marathon. The enthusiastic Colonel Papadiamantopoulos, who was to be the Olympic marathon starter, strengthened the two Greek trial races by entering likely men who had served in his regiment. One was a 24-year-old from the village of Amaroússion, Spiridon Louis.

Louis was from a working-class background, like most of the Greek marathon hopefuls and unlike the wealthy college athletes who were to dominate those first Olympics. For the marathon, it proved a crucial advantage. It often still is. The

family had a small business transporting barrels of water by mule or cart from a spring near their village into Athens, about eight miles away. The young Spiridon used to jog alongside, sometimes twice a day both ways. He may have been doing it for years—no one thought to ask him at the time. It's only now that we know how vital those early years of routine running can be.

The road Louis jogged from the village spring was not the course the marathon took to the Panathenaikon Stadium, but it followed much the same approach into the city. He knew the contours, the rough, stony road surfaces, and the local weather. Running cautiously in the second Greek selection trial on March 24, 1896, he had finished fifth out of 38 starters, seven minutes behind the winner, Ioannis Lavrentis, but in a time, 3:18:27, that would have been close to winning the previous selection trial. He was a contender.

The 17 Olympic runners were transported from Athens to Marathon the day before the race. Thirteen were Greek. Of the visitors, only one, the Hungarian Gyula Kellner, had long-distance experience. The other three had filled the top places in the 1,500 meters two days earlier. The winner, London-based Australian Edwin "Teddy" Flack,

Previous spread: After lying dormant for 2,000 years, the Olympic Games were revived in Athens in 1896. Admiring crowds packed the stadium, reconstructed in marble on the ancient model, with a long, narrow track.

Right: Frenchman Michel Bréal proposed a "marathon race" in the 1896 Olympic Games, and donated this silver cup to commemorate "the heroic messenger" of ancient legend. The cup was rediscovered nearly a hundred years later, modestly tucked away at the home where Spiridon Louis's descendants still lived.

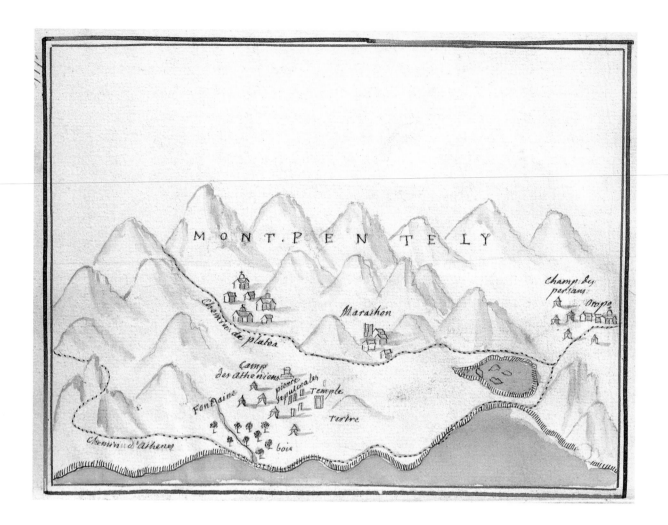

also won the 800 meters only two hours before they departed for Marathon. He was a good middle-distance and cross-country runner, in the lightly trained fashion of the time, but he had no idea of what lay ahead in 25 miles of running.

The next day, April 10, was cool with clear skies. Moments before 2 p.m. the runners stood at the bridge in Marathon in four short rows to hear the starter's speech. They wore shirts, drawers, and assorted caps, a few in national colors. Their bicycle attendants also waited, each ready to pedal behind his runner and provide refreshment and encouragement. Behind them Greek officials and soldiers on horseback completed what one observer called "an odd caravan of attendants." A few hundred people were watching. They thought they were at the commemoration of an ancient local story. In fact, they were witnessing the birth of something new and universal, beyond their wildest imaginings.

At the starter's pistol, the visiting track runners went out predictably fast, the rest of the field straggling behind. The course was relatively flat as they left the village and followed the seacoast road to Rafina. Albin Lermusiaux of France immediately led, his white gloves twinkling. The tall Flack followed, prancing along in his tasseled school cap, accompanied by a bicycling diplomat wearing a black bowler hat, and by the American runner-up from the 1,500 meters, Arthur Blake. Lermusiaux raced away with Gallic verve and by nine miles had a lead said to be almost two miles (though these estimated times and distances are less than reliable).

The Greeks, with experience of the distance, chose their pace more carefully. Lavrentis, the second trial winner, was closest to the foreigners at first, but faded and dropped out, to be replaced by Kharilaos Vasilakos, the first trial winner, and Spiridon Louis. They knew the real race had not yet begun.

At a *taverna* at Pikermi at 13 miles, just after the uphill began, Louis accepted a glass of wine and cheerfully announced to the crowd that he would win. That would soon look less wildly optimistic than it seemed. By 16 miles, Lermusiaux was struggling to hold the remnant of his huge early lead. He was only just able to relish the triumphal arch and crown of leaves provided for the race leader by the villagers of Harvati. But the dark monster of the marathon lurked on the next uphill, as it has awaited so many of us since.

Left: An early map depicts the route from Marathon to Athens, following the coastline for much of the route, rather than the the steeper way through the mountains. The coastal route was also used for the 2004 Olympic race.

Lermusiaux staggered to a stop and lay down for a rub with alcohol by his attendant. When he tried to resume, he knew he wouldn't be able to finish.

Flack, the debonair Australian, sensing a third victor's wreath, skipped into the lead. That news, carried by a frantic cyclist to the finish, produced a groan of disappointment from the packed crowds in the Panathenaikon Stadium. They had been watching yet more American victories on the track. They were waiting for a Greek.

If there had been a giant TV screen to show the race in progress, they might have had more hope. According to the official report, Vasilakos and Louis were within reach of the foreigners and running well. Louis was well used to pacing himself. He did it every day. Even when Vasilakos slowed on the last of the uphills, Louis waited. Then, at 21 miles, he moved quickly away from his teammate, surprised Flack, and took a short lead.

Flack's astonishment at how quickly Louis closed the big gap has fostered a number of stories about cheating. The fact is that the "peasant," as British and French journalists called Louis, was better prepared for the marathon than a well-educated London accountant. When someone hits the wall in the marathon, a two-minute lead can evaporate in less than a mile. It still happens at the front of major marathons. It happened to Flack.

Louis bided his time. At 23 miles, not far from his home village, his girlfriend Eleni was waiting. She gave him some orange segments, and no doubt words of love and encouragement. Doubly inspired, and downhill, Spiridon increased the pace. This long slope to the city was familiar terrain, as it was to Pheidippides before him. Flack folded. He soon joined Lermusiaux in the horse-drawn sag wagons.

Louis ran steadily toward the ancient city, escorted by screaming boys and treading on flower petals tossed by girls. He was minutes clear of the next runner, who was also a Greek. A cyclist pedaling ahead cried *Ellene! Ellene!* ("Greek! Greek!") At the city boundary, a cannon was fired to announce the leader's approach. The starter, who had ridden the long course on horseback, galloped to the finish to inform King Georgios that a Greek was winning. Word spread round the stadium, packed with fervent crowds estimated between 60,000 and 125,000.

The pole vault came to a stop. Bigger things were happening. "A man wearing white, sunburnt, and covered in perspiration, is seen to enter," wrote the official Olympic reporter. The

Right: When Spiridon Louis ran into the stadium to win the first Olympic marathon, the ecstatic Greek crowds threw handkerchiefs, flowers and jewelry, while the excited crown prince ran alongside, brandishing his hat in jubilant abandon. The marathon was born.

crowd rose to their feet, cheering wildly. Every woman waved a handkerchief or fan. Every man waved his hat. The two royal princes ran the length of the stadium alongside Louis, also flourishing their hats. Even the king "nearly ripped off the visor of his naval uniform cap in waving it wildly."

The crowd "went mad for joy" as Louis broke the string across the track at the top of the tightly curved bend (2:58:50 for about 25 miles). He stopped at last, bowed to the king, and stood for the band to play the Greek national anthem. After that pause, the jubilation was even more passionate. "It was a moment I could never have imagined. The crowds were calling my name. Flowers and bouquets were raining down on me and hats were flying in the air," Louis told the French sports paper, *L'Equipe*.

"Enthusiasm swelled like an unstoppable wave," wrote Pierre de Coubertin, the founder of the modern Olympics. It swelled again seven minutes later, when Vasilakos entered the stadium in second place (3:06:03). His moment was briefer than Louis's lifelong fame. Nothing could diminish the zeal for Spiridon. It was national ecstasy. He was showered with gifts that included meals, clothing, haircuts, jewelry, watches, a sewing machine,

Left: Greece honors one of its own. Humble water-carrier Spiridon Louis, in full national costume, accepts gold medal adulation.

and from the king, a new horse and cart for the water-carrying business.

To the promoters of the new Olympics, Louis's victory proved that the movement's internationalism would foster, not diminish, national pride. That was a big issue in 1896. It is perhaps ironic that when Louis briefly emerged to be honored at a later Olympics, it was in 1936, in Berlin, the most nationalistic of all Games. Probably he never knew what a crucial inspiration, for better and for worse, his victory was. We can see now that his triumph transformed two unlikely experiments —Olympic sport and the marathon race—into two of the most remarkable, and still most positive phenomena of the 20th century and beyond. Spiridon Louis struck the spark. Everyone in Athens that day was lit by the flame, and carried it home with them.

The first "marathon race" outside Greece was only four months later, on July 19, 1896, a prize-money event near Paris. On September 20 came the first amateur marathon, when 30 men ran, walked and floundered through 25 miles of muddy roads from Stamford, Connecticut, to Columbia Oval in New York. Similar races imitating the point-to-point "hero's journey" into the heart of a city were run in Hungary, Norway, and Denmark in October 1896. Most portentously, on

April 19, 1897, 15 runners lined up at Ashland, Massachusetts, under the auspices of the Boston Athletic Association, to run 25 miles into Boston. The New England city chose Patriot's Day to link the story of Pheidippides with America's own legend of a heroic messenger, the revolutionary ride of Paul Revere.

How the tidy 25 miles (40 km) of these first marathons was transmuted into the illogical 26 miles, 385 yards of today is one of the more convoluted stories in sport. It began with the devastating eruption of Mount Vesuvius in March 1906. With all Italy reeling, the 1908 Olympic Games were moved from Rome to London. For the marathon race, the organizers quickly devised a course that again followed the "journey to the city" motif, running from the East Terrace of Windsor Castle to the White City Stadium at Hammersmith, West London. This meant extending the distance to about 26 miles. The runners were then required to complete most of one lap of the track to a line beneath the VIP spectators, notably Queen Alexandra. The official Olympic report states, "385 yards were run on the cinder track to the finish, below the Royal Box."

The Polytechnic Harriers club, which had responsibility for organizing the Olympic race, inaugurated its own annual Polytechnic Marathon in 1909, over a largely similar course from Windsor Castle, but finishing at the Stamford Bridge track, a few miles from White City. The distance of exactly 26 miles, 385 yards was used. Curious though it was, the "English marathon" distance was formally adopted as the standard for the Olympic marathon at Paris in 1924, a decision that perhaps reflects British influence in those years after World War I.

No wonder some marathon runners get cantankerous at about 25 miles. On the other hand, Mount Everest is 29,141 feet high. Sometimes tidy round figures are not the point.

In 1989, we were in Greece making a TV documentary about the marathon (*A Hero's Journey*) for a Greek producer. The greatest pleasure of the job was the long, late evening meals with the crew in local tavernas. One night, in Rafina, a little boy was running merrily around the tables. One man called out to encourage him, "Run! Be like Louis!" Our Greek interpreter confirmed what he had said. It is a common proverb, meaning, "Move quickly and succeed." In Greece, the name of Spiridon Louis is part of the language.

Left: Johnny Hayes of the United States receives the 1908 Olympic trophy from Queen Alexandra.

Right: Runners at the 1908 Olympic Marathon. The race began at Windsor Castle, where the Princess of Wales sent them on their way to the White City Stadium, to finish beneath the Royal Box of Queen Alexandra.

05

MAPPING THE COURSE

THE STRANGE DISTANCE OF 26.2 is now immutable, and marathon organizers make measurement errors at their peril. The distance is forever. That aside, mapping a new course is an exercise in creativity, with countless variations possible. Adventurous runners today can even choose courses that go wholly or partly off paved roads, like the Great Wall, Deadwood Mickelson Trail in South Dakota, or Boulder Backroads marathons. In planning a more conventional course, inventiveness and runner preferences must be complemented by skills in local politics and the ability to negotiate with police, residents, shoppers, churchgoers, and a thousand other legitimate users of the roads. There is remarkable goodwill everywhere toward marathons, but it is not unlimited.

Among the wide range of possible course designs, three are probably most attractive to runners. The first is the original point-to-point "Pheidippides journey," ideally finishing at a significant destination that enhances the runners' sense of heroic achievement. Apart from the long-established Athens and Boston courses, good modern examples include Niagara (which crosses an international border and finishes in the spray of the falls), Grandma's in Minnesota (which takes its name from the famous restaurant at the finish line) and Napa Valley (which follows part of the historic Silverado Trail).

Scenery dictates many of the increasingly popular courses that run around lakes, along shorelines or through areas of natural beauty. The crossover between marathon running and destination tourism is shaping the modern sport. A survey of advertisements aimed at attracting runners to marathons showed the most common buzzword was "scenic," followed by "memorable," "beautiful," "fun," and "fast," in that order.

The third popular course model dates from 1900, when the Parisian organizers of the second modern Olympics laid out a marathon described as a *Tour de Paris*. That devious route through city back streets proved an infamous failure, with many runners hopelessly lost and the winner suspected of having benefited from local knowledge. But the idea was a good one, and many of today's greatest marathons offer sightseeing tours of major cities. To rubberneck in front of cheering crowds around a big city closed for our private pleasure is one of the privileges of being a modern marathon runner.

Then there are the lifetime experiences—that word "memorable" in the race ads. Runners love the opportunity to run across a major bridge (New Orleans, San Francisco, Sydney), or cross international borders (Detroit, Istanbul, Niagara), or visit a national capital (Canberra, Ottawa, Washington) or tour a wild animal game park (Safaricom), or

Previous spread: The Honolulu Marathon in Hawaii encompasses the famous Diamond Head, where a stunning dormant volcano lurks alongside the runners who pass by every December.

Right: The endurancelife Coastal Marathon route was designed to coincide with part of the famous South West Coastal Path (the longest public path in Britain, at over 600 miles). The coastal geography makes for stunning views and an extremely challenging course.

START / FINISH

START POINT

PRAWLE POINT

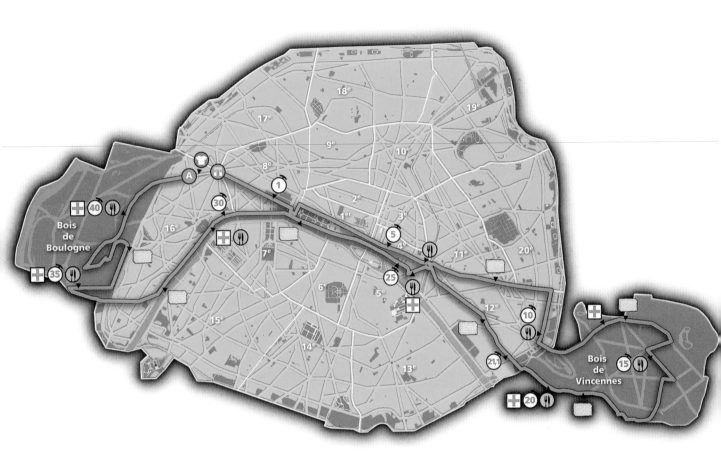

witness natural wonders (the midnight sun in Norway), or face the extra challenge of running the distance through Antarctic snows, or Saharan sand, or thin Himalayan air.

We also, perversely, want to run faster. The marathon remains a serious competitive sport as well as a mass-participation activity. Some courses are designed for speed, offering flat terrain, smooth road surface, little camber, temperate weather, and often an out-and-back route to minimize wind effect. Amsterdam, Christchurch, Fukuoka, Kosice, and Rotterdam are some of the classics. "Criterium" courses, where the same fast loop is repeated several times, are increasingly popular with elite runners, spectators and TV directors.

Part of the sport's appeal is that every marathon is, in the fullest sense, special. Every course is local, every race day is subject to the vagaries of wind and weather, every runner's experience in every race every year is unique. Bragging rights about best times always include qualifiers: "But that was into a headwind," "I never did one in cool conditions," "There was construction that messed up the road for nearly a mile." All these variables are a challenge to legislators charged with maintaining fairness. Selecting national teams is a recurring nightmare, since it's impossible to design a trial race exactly anticipating the conditions that

will be encountered in the championship. Only recently have marathon times been recognized as official world records, and then only with criteria that eliminate performances that benefit from elevation loss or following wind.

The one thing that can be confidently legislated is the distance. Dedicated work in the last half of the 20th century by skilled enthusiasts such as Alan Jones and John Jewell in the UK, Ted Corbitt in the US, and Norm Patenaude in Canada led to techniques and technology that at last ensured accurate measurement. Jones replaced time-consuming surveyors' methods with a simple device that counts the revolutions of a calibrated bicycle wheel. It is now known as the Clain Jones counter, after Alan's son who took over the assembly process. The Association of International Marathons and Road Races (AIMS) has a team of expert measurement administrators who maintain standards around the world. The rare cases of inaccurate measurement enrich marathon folklore and blog sites. But almost always, whatever the effects of hills, crowds, footing, or weather, you can be sure you have run the right distance: 26.2 miles/ 42.2 km. The distance is forever.

Left: The route of the Paris Marathon is a classic "city tour."

Following spread: The route at the Blackmores Sydney Marathon ends with a view of the Sydney Opera House.

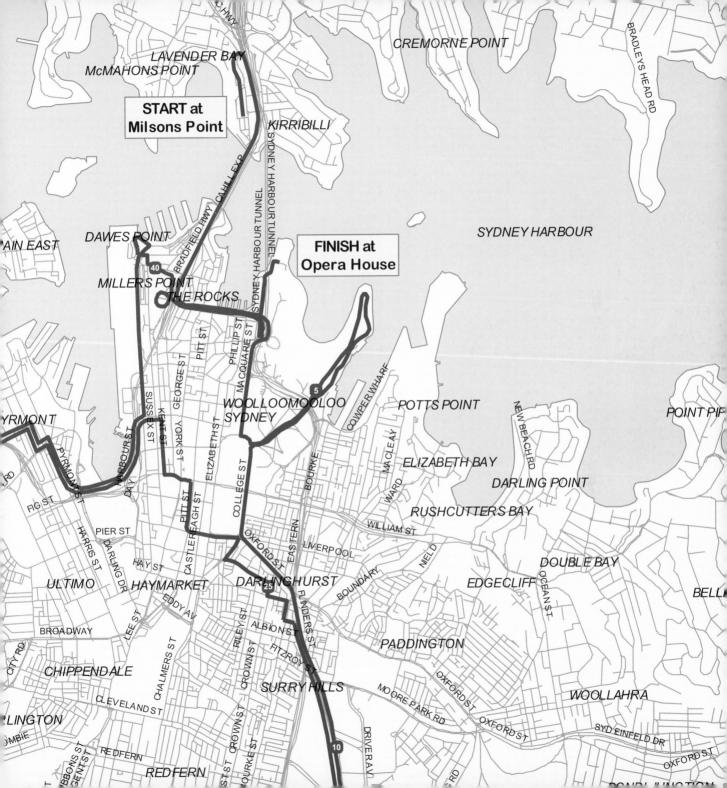

"If you want to run, run a mile. If you want to experience another life, run a marathon." —EMIL ZATOPEK | "…by adopting the marathon lifestyle you can confront your own lions, be your own hero, fight your own battles, challenge yourself." —RICHARD BENYO, *MAKING THE MARATHON YOUR EVENT* | "I have run a marathon. Okay, so it's been done before. But not by me." —CLIFF TEMPLE, *CHALLENGE OF THE MARATHON* | "It's like tacking PhD at the end of your name, getting married, having a baby. Your life will never again be quite the same, and regardless of what the future brings, you can look back and say, 'I finished a marathon.'" —HAL HIGDON, *MARATHON* | "There are only three winners: The one who competes with himself, the one who crosses the finish line first, and the one who finishes the race." —SRI CHINMOY, *THE OUTER RUNNING AND THE INNER RUNNING* | "I've learned that finishing a marathon…isn't just an athletic achievement. It's a state of mind; a state of mind that says anything is possible." —JOHN HANC, *THE ESSENTIAL RUNNER* | "And now I'm finishing a 26-mile race. Damn! This is better than winning an Emmy!" —OPRAH WINFREY | "The most important thing is not to win but to take part, just as in life the most important thing is not the triumph but the struggle. The essential thing is not to have conquered but to have fought well." —THE OLYMPIC CREED | "I ran the marathon for my 60th birthday; I wanted to do something outrageous and impossible." —KAYE DURLAND SPILKER (FIRST-TIME MARATHONER) |

06

MOTIVATIONS

"I started running at age 72 because I was tired of all the boring talk about funerals."—RUTH ROTHFARB (WHO RAN HER FIRST MARATHON AT AGE 81) | "I know of no more encouraging fact than the unquestionable ability of man to raise himself through conscious endeavor."—HENRY DAVID THOREAU | "We run because we like it, Through the broad bright land."—C.H. SORLEY, "SONG OF THE UNGIRT RUNNERS" | "If modern runners were drawn around a campfire in a warm African night, they would, like any Bushmen after a hunt, poke the embers and relive the run all the way to the finish line."—BERND HEINRICH, WHY WE RUN | "We run, not because we think it is doing us good, but because we enjoy it and cannot help ourselves. It also does us good because it helps us to do other things better. It gives a man the chance to bring out power that might otherwise remain locked away inside himself. The urge to struggle lies latent in everyone."—ROGER BANNISTER, FIRST FOUR MINUTES | "I did the marathon because everyone said I couldn't."—JEAN DRISCOLL (EIGHT-TIME WHEELCHAIR WINNER OF THE BOSTON MARATHON) | "Every one of my runners is disabled in some way. For them, the race is a double challenge that many of them never imagined they could meet. Whatever they discover along the way has been inside them all along. What the marathon does is introduce them to themselves."—DICK TRAUM (AMPUTEE, FOUNDER OF ACHILLES TRACK CLUB), A VICTORY FOR HUMANITY | "Competitive running is a metaphor for the unresting aspiration of the human spirit."—ROGER

ROBINSON, *HEROES AND SPARROWS* | "I guess you could say I'm competitive, but really there aren't a lot of people in my age group."—BERTHA McGRUDER, AGE 77, OLDEST COMPETITOR IN THE MORE MARATHON | "The marathon is an art; the marathoner is an artist."—COACH KIYOSHI NAKAMURA | "The marathon is my only girlfriend. I give her everything I have."—TOSHIHIKO SEKO | "For all of us, the miracle isn't that we finish, the miracle is that we have the courage to start."—JOHN "THE PENGUIN" BINGHAM | "It doesn't matter how slow you go, as long as you do not stop."—LAO-TZU | "Successful marathoners must lose their cool, and allow this irrational, animal consciousness to take over."—BILL RODGERS | "Racing is where I have to face the truth about myself."—JOE HENDERSON | "Our thoughts and beliefs are the blueprints from which we create our physical reality."—LORRAINE MOLLER | "Running is a way of life for me, just like brushing my teeth. If I don't run for a few days, I feel as if something's been stolen from me."—JOHN A. KELLEY | "All those grand thoughts of running your best time are draining away. All you want to be sure of is finishing. You're scared that you won't finish."—NORMAN HARRIS, *CHAMPION OF NOTHING* | "Do most of us want life on the same calm level as a geometrical problem? Certainly we want our pleasures more varied with both mountains and valleys of emotional joy, and marathoning furnishes just that."—CLARENCE DEMAR, *MARATHON* |

07

HEROES 1896–1956

Kharilaos Vasilakos Greece, b. 1871
Best time: 3:06:03 (c. 25 miles, 1896)

He won the first marathon in history, the Greek trial on the Marathon to Athens course, March 10, 1896. Only a month later he ran 12 minutes faster in the first Olympic marathon, to finish second—and be forgotten. A respected senior customs officer, he lived to the age of 92.

Spiridon Louis Greece, b. 1873
Best time: 2:58:50 (c. 25 miles, 1896)

His undying place in sports history and as a Greek national legend came with his victory by a 7-minute margin in the first Olympic marathon. A water carrier and part-time soldier, his daily 14-mile walk/jog alongside the cart gave him stamina and pace judgment.

Len Hurst England, b. 1871
Best time: 2:26:48 (c. 40 km, 1900)

Twenty minutes faster than Louis when he won the first post-Athens "marathon"—40 kilometers for professional runners near Paris, July 19, 1896. He won the same race twice more and excelled in longer distance events. He combined hard walk/run training with his arduous trade of brickmaker.

Billy Sherring Canada, b. 1878
Best time: 2:41:31 (c. 25 miles, 1900)

Won the second "Olympic" marathon in Athens, the "Interim Games" of 1906. A horseracing tip gave the railway brakeman his fares to Greece. Of Irish heritage, he won the Hamilton Round the Bay (19 miles) twice, and was the 1900 Boston runner-up.

Tom Longboat Canada (Onondaga Nation), b. 1887
Best time: 2:45:05 (professional, 1908)

They called him "the greatest distance runner the world has ever seen," when he won Boston at age 19. He was defeated by extreme heat in the 1908 Olympics, but as a professional he beat Dorando Pietri twice and English star Alfred Shrubb once.

Dorando Pietri Italy, b. 1885
Best time: 2:44:20.4 (professional, 1909)

Leading the 1908 London Olympic marathon into the stadium, the little pastry cook from Carpi collapsed five times in that roaring cauldron; he was helped to the finish line, and therefore disqualified. His drama inspired global "marathon mania." As a professional, he won 17 of 22 races.

Johnny Hayes United States, b. 1886
Best time: 2:41:49 (professional, 1910)
Hayes won the 1908 Olympic title by cool pace judgment on a hot day, the only runner who finished strong. He had won at Yonkers and St. Louis, and placed well at Boston. He went on to success as a professional, one of many great early marathoners of Irish heritage.

Henri St. Yves France, b. 1888
Best time: 2:40:50.6 (professional, 1909)
Spectators jeered when the 5-foot-tall chauffeur scuttled into the lead of the "Marathon Derby," New York, April 3, 1909. Over five dizzying laps per mile, he beat the four greats (Pietri, Hayes, Longboat, and Shrubb) by 5 minutes, in the fastest time ever to that point, repeating the feat a month later.

Ken McArthur South Africa (b. Ireland), b. 1882
Best time: 2:42:58 (1910)
Unbeaten in South Africa, then a marathon stronghold, McArthur overcame unexpected 86°F heat in Stockholm to win the 1912 Olympic marathon. His 1910 time for the "London distance" of 26.2 miles was the best to date.

Hannes Kolehmainen Finland, b. 1889
Best time: 2:32:35.8 (1920)
The first Flying Finn broke the world record in the Olympic marathon by 3 minutes, on a course that was 607 yards longer than the standard 26.2 miles, having won three Olympic races in 1912. Based in New York 1913–1920, he set many US records, but still competed for Finland.

Albin Stenroos Finland, b. 1889
Best time: 2:29:40 (1926)
His powerful second half gave him the 1924 Paris Olympic victory by 6 minutes. In a long but uneven career, he ran no marathons from 1909–1924, though he set world marks at 20 and 30 kilometers. The sturdy woodworker was runner-up at Boston in 1926.

Clarence DeMar United States, b. 1888
Best time: 2:34:48 (1930)
"Mr. DeMarathon" won Boston seven times (1911–1930). Oldest winner at age 41, he ran it 32 times (1910–1954), always at a high level for his age. A three-time Olympian, winning the bronze medal in 1924, he pioneered high-mileage training, and wrote *Marathon* in 1937.

Boughera El Ouafi **France (b. Algeria),**
b. 1898
Best time: 2:32:57 (1928)
The first African-born runner to win the
Olympic marathon, the Arabian date grower
had run many desert miles as a French army
courier. A master of peaking and pace, in 1928
he beat the most international field ever
assembled, and later ran well as a professional.

Juan Zabala **Argentina, b. 1911**
Best time: 2:31:36 (1932)
The first Olympic marathon champion from
South America, he still holds the record of
youngest winner—at 20. With four close pur-
suers at Los Angeles, Zabala pushed so close
to exhaustion that Damon Runyon called him
"a modern reincarnation of Pheidippides." It
was the peak of an uneven career.

Sam Ferris **Great Britain (b. Northern**
Ireland), b. 1900
Best time: 2:31:55 (1932)
This lively air force serviceman placed in the
top 10 in three Olympic marathons and was
only 19 seconds from the gold in 1932, his
fastest race. A hero for sustained excellence,
he was Polytechnic champion eight times,
and won 12 of 21 marathons.

Sohn Kee-Chung (Kitei Son) **Japan**
(b. Korea), b. 1912
Best time: 2:26:42 (1935)
In occupied Korea, Sohn was forced to accept a
Japanese name and affiliation. He set a world
record in 1935 and won gold in the 1936
Berlin Olympics. In 1988, carrying the flame
into the Seoul stadium, Sohn at last claimed
Olympic honor in his own name and nationality.

Ellison "Tarzan" Brown **United States**
(Narragansett Nation), b. 1914
Best time: 2:27:29.6 (1940)
Labeled "Tarzan" by the newspapers, he was
a tactically astute, resolute, and popular runner who won Boston twice, setting a course
record in 1939. In the 1936 Olympics he was
running with the leaders when pain from a
hernia stopped him.

Johnny A. Kelley **United States, b. 1907**
Best time: 2:28:18 (1940)
The greatest marathoner ever for lifetime
excellence through all age groups, to 80-plus.
At Boston he was legendary, winning twice,
placing top ten 18 times, and finishing the
course an astonishing 58 times. At Yonkers,
he ran 29 times, winning twice, and was a
three-time Olympian (18th, 1936).

Gérard Côté Canada, b. 1913
Best time: 2:28:25 (1943)

For all his panache and post-race cigars, the debonair Quebecker was a rugged competitor. He won Boston four times (1940-48), placed top 10 on nine other occasions, and won marathons in Canada and Los Angeles. The war deprived him of his best Olympic years; he was 17th in 1948.

Stylianos Kyriakides Greece, b. 1910
Best time: 2:29:27 (1946)

He embodied the revival of a war-ravaged world, especially starving Greece, with his emotional win at Boston in 1946. Like Pheidippides, he carried a message: "Win or die." He had placed 11th at the 1936 Berlin Olympics, an achievement that twice saved his life under Nazi occupation.

Yun Bok Suh Korea, b. 1923
Best time: 2:25:39 (1947)

American soldiers in Korea raised the expenses for two young runners, coached by Olympic champion Sohn Kee-Chung, to run at Boston in 1947. As a symbol of revival it matched Kyriakides's when the 115-pound Suh outran an Olympic-quality field for a world-record victory.

Delfo Cabrera Argentina, b. 1919
Best time: 2:26:42.4 (1952)

The multiple South American track champion finished fast in his first marathon, the 1948 London Olympics, passing the exhausted Belgian Etienne Gailly in the stadium. Eight minutes faster in 1952, he placed sixth. A teacher, he became president of Argentina's Olympic Association.

Jack (John) Holden England, b. 1907
Best time: 2:32:13.2 (1950)

After racing internationally from 1929 (International Cross-Country), he moved to the marathon at age 39 and for five years was among the world's best. One of the greatest all-time over-40 runners, he won the 1950 European and Empire marathons, despite blisters and dog attack in Auckland.

Veikko Karvonen Finland, b. 1926
Best time: 2:18:56.4 (1956)

The consistent Finn led the world at the end of the era before 2:20 was broken. He won 14 of 34 marathons, including the European championship in 1954, and major victories at Boston, Enschede, Athens, and Fukuoka. He ended his long elite career with Olympic bronze in 1956.

RUNNING

AND

CROSS-COUNTRY RUNNING

By

ALFRED SHRUBB

With
32 Plates

2/6 NETT

"HEALTH &
STRENGTH" Lᵀᴰ
LONDON

08

TRAINING

There are many different kinds of training: long run, repetition, time trials.... These are all pieces of a puzzle. How you put the pieces together is the art of training.

—Kiyoshi Nakamura

MILLIONS OF YEARS AGO humans evolved as distance runners. It was one way of obtaining food. They were not as fast as the antelope they chased or the cheetah that was their rival in the hunt. But they had one unique advantage—they planned a long way ahead. When an antelope is startled, it escapes at full sprint speed. It never plans to save energy for a chase lasting many hours. It never practices stamina. But our early human ancestors could plan, imagine, and practice. In the words of biologist-runner-author Bernd Heinrich, "When they felt fatigue and pain, they did not stop, because their dream carried them still forward."

We train for the marathon because we still plan ahead. We are the only animals that understand the need to train now in order to run well in six months' time. It is a natural process. Watch a one-year-old learn to walk—staggering and stomping, testing balance and building strength, working and resting, repeatedly practicing to improve. That's what a marathon runner in training is doing.

The principle is simple. To improve at something, you progressively demand levels of performance from your body that it hasn't encountered before. This applies to swimming or dancing the tango as well as training for a marathon. Your body likes doing things well. It dislikes the discomfort of getting tired. So it will slowly learn to get better. It adapts. It is called stimulus and response, or adaptation to overload or stress. Add 5 minutes each week to your long run, and in time your body will adapt to running twice as far as it once could. Run 5 seconds a mile faster in your intervals, and soon you will be running faster in the race. Run hills, and you will be able to run hills.

Because we plan, we also make choices. The marathon requires a complex range of strengths and skills. The challenge of training is to develop those strengths and skills you will benefit from most. And "benefit" can mean a thousand different things. A newly recruited charity runner aiming to jog and walk the distance with a friendly group has training needs very different from a sub-3-hour competitive runner aiming to take 5 minutes off his or her best time.

Legendary Japanese coach Kiyoshi Nakamura's "art of training" thus begins with setting your goals. Then plan—or ask your coach to plan—the training that will fulfill them. Take into account

Previous spread: The first great training book for distance runners was Alfred Shrubb's 1909 manual. The pioneer of intensive training that mixes distance and speed work, Shrubb, an English rural builder who became a multiple world-record breaker, is described on the title page as "The World's Greatest Pedestrian."

Right: "The athlete should now order his life on a set system," wrote Shrubb. Shrubb was disciplined, training twice daily in the weeks leading to his world record 10 miles in November 1904.

Date.	Morning work.	Afternoon work.	Weight stripped.
6th Oct. ...	3 miles fairly slow	6 miles at decent pace... ...	122 lbs.
7th Oct. ...	4 miles good pace	5 miles good pace	120 lbs.
8th Oct. ...	4 miles good pace	Wet, did not go out	120 lbs.
9th Oct. ...	Sunday	... ...	122 lbs.
10th Oct...	3 miles fairly fast	3 miles slow	121 lbs.
11th Oct...	2 miles fast	6 miles slow	120½ lbs.
12th Oct...	Did not run	6 miles medium	120 lbs.
13th Oct...	3 miles good pace	4 miles medium	119¾ lbs.
14th Oct...	5 miles steady	Did not run	120 lbs.
15th Oct...	Brisk walk	3 miles fast	119½ lbs.
16th Oct...	Sunday	... ...	121 lbs.
17th Oct...	8 miles steady	2 miles fast burst	12¾ lbs.
18th Oct...	4 miles good pace	2 miles (9 min. 18 secs.) ...	120 lbs.
19th Oct...	Did not run	10-mile trial (51 min. 10 secs.)...	119 lbs.
20th Oct...	5 miles steady	Did not run	118½ lbs.

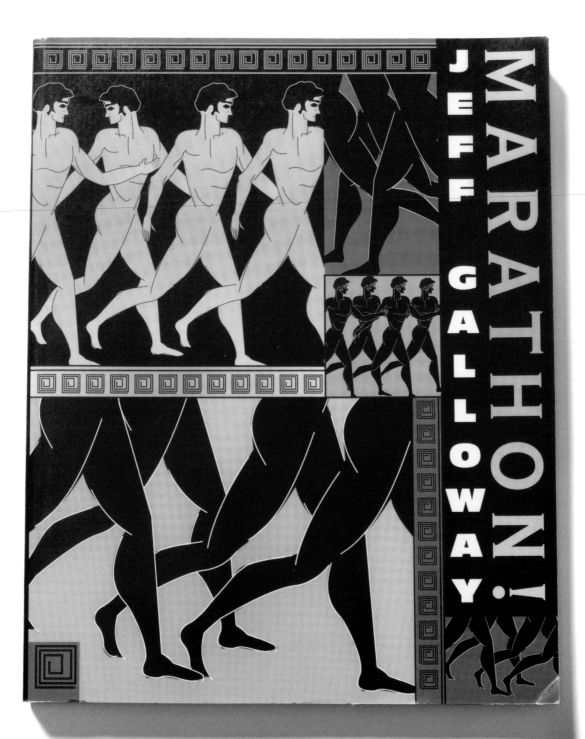

the terrain and weather you will meet, the abilities of the body you have been given, and the time and energy you have available.

The base is always a lot of running. Pheidippides was an "all-day runner." Spiridon Louis walked or jogged daily with the family water cart. Early in the modern era, when it was fashionable to fear "going stale," Clarence DeMar showed the benefits of running nearly a hundred miles a week, with seven victories at Boston.

Then comes speed. More than a hundred years ago, multiple record breaker Alfred Shrubb trained by mixing short, fast runs with longer endurance runs and long walks. In the 1950s, Jim Peters continued that pragmatic English tradition. He trained with a track runner's intensity, twice a day at 5-minute miles, and broke the world marathon record four times.

The final element is planning. Preparing the body to race needs to be done progressively. Shrubb meticulously recorded his training and learned from and shared the results; his books were deservedly influential for many decades. The master of long-term thinking was New Zealand guru Arthur Lydiard, who showed Olympic medalists and joggers alike how to plan ahead, like prehistoric hunters. First lay down a basis of distance, he advised, then build strength by running up hills, and finally train

for speed. Nakamura and other great coaches acknowledged their debt to the Lydiard system.

A different kind of pioneer since the 1980s has been Jeff Galloway. In his training books, groups, camps, and on-line advice, he showed that it is permissible to do less, instead of more, making the marathon more accessible by encouraging people to alternate running with walking. Galloway runners aspire to finish marathons rather than excel in them.

The challenge is always finding the balance, the right plan. You are seeking the best way of extending the distance that you can last on the hunt, the best way to improve your speed as a hunter. Don't forget speed. Too many runners modestly delude themselves about their goals. Before a marathon they tell you they only want to finish. Afterward they castigate themselves for a slow time. Be honest. We almost all want to improve. So training should include some preparation for the pace you hope to race. If you worry about how hard it will be, go to the most beautiful area you know with your best running friends and have fun. If it still seems hard, remember those ancestors of ours chasing down the groceries.

We were meant and designed to run long and hard. Training for that is not an imposition, not artificial, not unnatural. It is in the essence of our being.

Left: Jeff Galloway, himself an Olympian, made the marathon distance achievable for thousands of people by advocating the concept of walking breaks.

Following spread: "Advice for beginners" in Shrubb's book. In a later chapter, Shrubb advises a weekly 16-mile run, and in the weeks before the race "lengthen your run to twenty miles or even twenty-five miles...either twice a week or three times a fortnight."

condition and not to have strained himself in any way, repeating the experiment once or twice during his first year.

The danger which he has chiefly to guard against will be any risk of "over-doing" it, either in strength or spirit. Early defeats may dishearten him, and too much continued effort at "getting home first," before he has come to his full powers, may work some constitutional damage which can never afterwards be repaired.

TRAINING FOR BEGINNERS.

Now, a long-distance runner, or a beginner who aspires to become such, must bear in mind that the distance which he will be called upon most frequently to negotiate is ten miles, and so all, or the majority, of his initial preparation and training must be devoted towards developing his powers to *staying* that distance in good condition.

Should he discover, after a while, that he is not cut out for success over this trying course, well, the following system will not have hurt him in any way.

He will soon be enabled to find out if he is better qualified to shine as a mile, two-mile, three-mile, or four-mile runner, and can abandon his previous ambitions and set himself to win fame as a mile champion, or at one or other of the middle distances.

Let him commence with covering two or three miles three times every week, say, in the following order: 2, 3, 2 (but this is in no way arbitrary; it won't hurt him to run the longer distance if he feels fit and well for it).

For three weeks these runs should be kept up, and the distances should be covered three times each week, say, two miles twice and three miles once.

Then, for the next fortnight, he should go out for a run again thrice a week, but the distance now should be over either four, five, or six miles, the longest stretch to be covered certainly once during the fortnight.

AFTER ONE HUNDRED YARDS.

(*Settling down.*)

[*Facing p.* 30

09

RUNNING FOR YOUR LIFE

MARATHON RUNNERS have always known the body never lies. Despite their own exhaustion and dire stories of ruined health, runners have felt in every fiber the long-term benefits of their extraordinary exercise. They ignored the old-time doctors who warned they would enlarge or strain the heart, prolapse the uterus and inflict arthritis. They disregarded the public that scorned them as eccentric masochists, and they openly defied the athletic bureaucrats who tried to restrict them in the name of protection. And in the end they won. The message they carried from Marathon to the world was that running is not only good for you—it is great for you.

Old fears delayed the message for nearly a century. When "marathon mania" briefly swept the world, and especially the United States, after Dorando Pietri's collapse in the 1908 Olympics, tens of thousands watched marathons, outdoors and in smoke-filled indoor arenas, in the juicy hope of witnessing pain and exhaustion. At a time when even top contenders were inexperienced and under-trained, dramatic reverses and serious collapse were common. An exhausted runner is always a disturbing sight, and the *New York Times* was prompted to issue its now-infamous 1909 declaration: "Every man who undertakes the running of 26 miles weakens his heart and shortens his life. For the great majority of adults particularly in an urban population, to take part in a Marathon race is to risk serious and permanent injury to health, with immediate death a danger not very remote."

Medical knowledge was primitive in many ways. No one understood that a few more miles in training, some patient pace judgment, and a cup or two of tap water are all that most runners need to reach the finish safely. One doctor who examined Pietri after his collapse pronounced that his heart had been displaced by half an inch. How he knew its exact location beforehand has never been explained. But that kind of primal fear of exhaustion, and the inhibitions of a society preoccupied with propriety, soon frightened the world off the marathon. The sport became confined to a small number of diehards who had discovered its addictive rewards. Their small numbers contributed to the mystique of danger.

Hard exercise has always had its adherents. Long before anyone knew about metabolic rates, the 18th-century Scottish novelist and surgeon Tobias Smollett wrote, "We should sometimes increase the motion of the machine, to unclog the wheels of life." Every generation since the Industrial Revolution has produced its own cult of health and fitness, from the Lake District hikes

Previous spread: Dr. Ernst van Aaken was the first scientist to put his reputation on the line and declare that women were naturally suited for endurance running. Van Aaken lived to see the women's marathon event included in the Olympic Games, thanks in great measure to his medical data.

Right: A collapsed Dorando Pietri is helped across the finish line at the 1908 Olympic marathon. This graphic image solidified the notion that marathon running pushes the body to dangerously unnatural extremes.

Ernst van Aaken / Karl Lennartz

DAS LAUFBUCH DER FRAU

MEYER & MEYER VERLAG

of the Romantic poets through the "muscular Christianity" of the Victorians, to Charles "you too can have a body like mine" Atlas, and the state-sponsored notions of physical and racial purity that reached their extreme in 1930s Germany. Virile masculinity and svelte womanhood were the usual ideals, achieved by vigorous exercise and fresh air.

Running became part of the lives of hundreds of thousands of World War II soldiers. Men learned the progressive effects of a regular training regime, how to pace themselves for the long haul, take water, and grease their boots. Many returned home, not to the hard agrarian work of earlier generations, but to a mechanized and largely sedentary world. Although reservists were required to keep fit, those who left the military often missed the hard-body life of wartime.

Army doctors were among the first to recognize the importance of exercise in rehabilitation. If it worked for wound recovery, why wouldn't it work for, say, heart attack recovery? In 1955 Dr. Paul Dudley White prescribed such radical treatment for a cardiac patient who was one of the greatest war veterans—President Dwight D. Eisenhower. A thankful Eisenhower created the President's Council on Youth Fitness in 1956, challenging millions of American school children to be fit. For many future marathon runners, their first timed running event was the annual 600-yard run at school.

The even more radical thought that vigorous exercise might also be a preventative had also emerged. In 1953, Dr. Jeremy Morris published a seminal study that revealed that British bus conductors, who had to run up and down the stairs of double-decker buses many times a day to collect fares, had significantly lower rates of heart attack than their drivers, who sat for long hours at the wheel. In the sixties, Arthur Lydiard, Bill Bowerman, Ken Cooper and Ernst van Aaken applied this thinking to the sport of long-distance running and began a revolution in exercise physiology and preventative health treatment.

In just one week in 1960, tiny New Zealand won three extraordinary Olympic long-distance running medals. The runners all lived in one suburban neighborhood. Their coach, ex-marathon champion Arthur Lydiard, maintained that running was good for everybody—even, and maybe especially, for post-cardiac patients. He proved it with a dramatically successful program of rehabilitative "jogging," and wrote about it, with Garth Gilmour, in *Run for Your Life*.

One person Lydiard inspired was the already legendary University of Oregon coach Bill Bowerman. On a visit to Lydiard in New Zealand, Bowerman found himself outrun by middle-aged recent heart attack victims. Back in the US, he wrote *Jogging* with Dr. Waldo Harris, aiming it at those seeking weight-loss and improved health as well as recuperation. The time was right. The book

continued on page 84

Left: Van Aaken's early women's running book is considered a classic.

Following spread: At left, the modern "running boom" had many beginnings, including a whole generation of young World War II soldiers. At right, school kids in the fifties took part in fitness training, including timed running events, thanks to Eisenhower's President's Council on Youth Fitness.

sold over a million copies and launched the running-for-everyone boom.

US Air Force physician Kenneth Cooper began running in 1960 to regain the fitness he had lost in medical school. When the air force sent him to Harvard for further study, he trained for the 1962 Boston Marathon. He was 30 when he met and ran with 54-year-old Johnny Kelley, who astonished him with his level of fitness. The marathon astonished him too. Cooper hit the wall at mile 18, suffered blisters, dehydration and depression, experienced euphoria, and reached the finish in tears. In short, he was hooked. Medically fascinated with what running could do for people's health, he conducted studies for the air force on how exercise could reduce heart attacks. In 1968, he wrote the best-selling *Aerobics*. When the book was excerpted in *Reader's Digest*, millions more encountered Cooper's points-based program, and many accepted his challenge to try running.

German physician Ernst van Aaken took ideas about the benefits of exercise one step further, by insisting that women would benefit equally from endurance training and had natural—even superior—capabilities. Fighting against thousands of years of myth, van Aaken was often scorned, but

he showed scientifically and anecdotally that women's smaller size and fat-burning abilities are advantageous in the long run. He backed up his research by coaching three women to world records in 10 years. His work was seminal in convincing the International Olympic Committee to add the women's marathon to the 1984 Olympic Games, as well as erasing fear of exercise for millions of women.

The running boom was on. Within 5 years, long established races such as Boston leapt from a few hundred starters to thousands, and new events such as New York, Chicago, Honolulu, London, Amsterdam and Berlin became crowded classics almost overnight. On the eve of the Boston Marathon in 1977, cardiologist and running guru Dr. George Sheehan told the runners, "First, be a good animal." And they were good animals—lean, strong, and hungry for a test that would take them to their mental and physical limits.

Sheehan was a great voice at just the pivotal moment when running seemed to change overnight from being feared as dangerously excessive into an exhilarating mass health movement. This reversal of medical myth is testimony not only to gutsy doctors such as Cooper, Sheehan,

Right: University of Oregon coach Bill Bowerman, here advising athlete Tom Smith, created winning athletes, winning teams, and innovative shoes.

and van Aaken, but also to the men and women runners who stubbornly conducted their own medical experiments on themselves—race after race, training week after training week—and knew how good it felt.

These runners, and the new ones who joined them in the boom years, soon learned that, in simple terms, the more you run, the healthier you get. This logic naturally left the roads littered with stress fractures, bum knees, anorexics, and burned-out cases, but it also led millions to become leaner, healthier, and happier. In an astonishingly short time, running, especially the marathon, had done more than any other health movement in history to "unclog the wheels of life."

Even the dedicated early marathoners would be surprised at the benefits that science now attributes to running. By strengthening the heart, running reduces the rate of heart disease. By pumping oxygen and antioxidants, it combats carcinogenic free radicals, and so reduces the incidence of many forms of cancer. By evacuating body waste promptly, it diminishes lingering toxins. By raising body temperature to fever level on a daily basis, it burns out infection. By stimulating sweating and increasing breath exchange, it eliminates toxins via the skin and expelled air. By releasing adrenaline, it flushes the system with disease-fighting white blood cells and immune substances. By reducing body weight, it counters the effects of obesity—stress on the heart, joints, lungs and muscles, and non-insulin dependent diabetes. By stimulating endorphins, it alleviates stress, counters depression, and enhances creativity and problem-solving. By strengthening bones, it radically reduces the incidence of osteoporosis. By maintaining strong blood flow and creating a positive self-image, it improves sexuality. Finally, by leaving the body fulfilled and tired, running helps maintain healthy sleep patterns.

Dr. Walter Bortz, a 70-plus marathon runner and leading authority on aging, has shown that even the miseries of old age can be significantly postponed and reduced by exercise. He concludes, "The renewal capacity of the human organism is almost boundless." By reducing the rate at which the aging body loses capacity (from an average 2 percent deterioration per year to an average .5 percent), running increases longevity and greatly improves the quality of later life. Running marathons is not the long sought Fountain of Youth, but it may be the nearest humanity has yet come to finding it.

Left: Runner's guru Dr. George Sheehan, shown preparing—at 49—for the Boston Marathon, with his son Michael, the youngest of his 12 children.

VITTEL
VITTEL
VITTEL
VITTEL
LE FIGARO
Cii Honeywell Bull
374
VITTEL
LE FIGARO
Cii Honeywell Bull
369
VITTEL

10

JOINING THE RACE

FOR A 19TH-CENTURY CREATION, the marathon was from the start remarkably open and egalitarian. With 3 miles to go in the Athens Olympics, the race was between a water carrier from a poor Greek village, an Athens public servant who would go on to be director of customs, and an upper-class London-based accountant representing Australia, who was attended by the butler of a senior diplomat. Few other activities in 1896 could put men of such diverse origins and class in close and equal contact.

This diverseness continued. Prominent in the early annals of the marathon are a Parisian woodworker from Luxembourg (Michel Théato), a Canadian railway brakeman (Billy Sherring), an Italian pastry cook (Dorando Pietri), a New York shipping clerk (Johnny Hayes), an orphaned French-Canadian ironworker living on an Iroquois reservation (Édouard Fabre), two Tswana tribesmen from South Africa, and the impoverished Onondaga Indian Tom Longboat, who ended his life as a garbage collector. Migrant Irish runners were prominent around the world. "The marathon was established as the sport of blue-collar athletes identified with minority groups," writes Pamela Cooper in her seminal social history, *The American Marathon*. It gave success to men such as Paul DeBruyn, who worked night shifts shoveling coal into the furnace of a New York hotel; Dave Komonen, an unemployed immigrant carpenter who sold his shoes after the 1933 Boston to buy a meal; Ted Corbitt, physiotherapist and the first African-American star; and Arnie Briggs, the shy little mailman with the injured back, whose oft-told Boston Marathon stories inspired a pioneering woman, Kathrine Switzer, to join the sport.

Jock Semple perhaps best represents the classic early marathoner. The Glasgow riveter's son took his running with him when he migrated to America. Running marathons sustained his sense of purpose through hardscrabble hungry years as an often unemployed carpenter. Good enough for the top 10 at Boston, he adopted that race as his lifetime passion. By 1947 he was co-race director, and his tiny basketball trainer's office at Boston Garden, redolent with menthol spirits and crammed with steam bath, massage table, and jangling phone, became "marathon central." Semple helped build Boston into a major event, and the marathon gave this rough-hewn boy from the shipyards international acclaim.

Previous spread: Older people, once dismissed as runners, are now welcomed and given special age categories. Those who run a race year after year—like these veterans from the *Cross du Figaro* in Paris—gain additional respect.

Right: One of the marathon's great early stars, Onondagan Tom Longboat (Cogwagee), won Boston at age 19 and became a leading professional after representing Canada in 1908.

T AND MARSH IN 5 MILE RACE,
IRISH-CANADIAN GAMES HAMILTON, ONT.

THE ROMANCE AND ACCESSIBILITY of the marathon quickly made it the world's most fully international sport. By 1920, Chile, Cuba, Egypt, India, Japan, and Serbia had all been represented in the Olympic marathon, as well as the familiar European and English-speaking nations. Early Olympic champions included Boughera El Ouafi, an Algerian date grower representing France, Juan Zabala, an Argentinian orphaned in infancy, and Sohn Kee-Chung, from a poor peasant village in occupied Korea, representing Japan.

The iconic moment in the marathon's global story came on September 10, 1960, on a Rome night damp with humidity. The Appian Way was lit by flares held on long poles by Italian soldiers. Waiting spectators peered into pools of yellow flickering light to glimpse the first runners. Suddenly they came, 2 minutes sooner than seemed possible in that searing heat, two together, both tall, lean, and dark-skinned. Astonishingly, the one in front was barefoot, running with a composed grace that looked almost dignified. The other, his shadow, was more angular and beginning to drift that first fatal half pace behind as they passed. They were Abebe Bikila of Ethiopia and Rhadi ben Abdesselem of Morocco, two

Africans heading the Olympic marathon for the first time. Bikila, still composed, would reach the Arch of Constantine alone, the first of the lithe and wondrous runners of Africa. On that dark night a new continent burst into the light.

FRAGMENTARY AND TANTALIZINGLY inconsistent reports say that a Greek woman called Melpomene or Stamata Revithi ran over the Athens Olympic course before or after the Olympic marathon in 1896. In 1926, Violet Piercy is credited with running the Polytechnic Marathon course in England in 3:40:22, a time that is accepted as the initial women's world record despite many uncertainties about how it was achieved (for example, the date is four months later than the Polytechnic Marathon, and the place listed, Chiswick, was not the finish point of the race in those years). So the story of how women joined the marathon must begin when Merry Lepper ran 3:37:07 on an uncertified course at Culver City, California, in 1963; Dale Greig recorded 3:27:45 at England's Isle of Wight in May 1964; and in New Zealand, Millie Sampson ran 3:19:33 in July 1964.

It was at Boston, though, that the story became high drama. Roberta Gibb, denied permission to

Left: An iconic moment in the globalization of the marathon occurs when a barefoot Ethiopian, Abebe Bikila (at left), runs into Rome to win the 1960 Olympic Marathon.

run the 1966 race, slipped in after the start, and ran a remarkable 3:21:40, beating nearly two-thirds of the men. Despite national publicity, officials insisted she was an interloper. But a year later when journalists on the officials' bus showed Jock Semple a "girl" wearing numbers in his race, his short fuse instantly ignited.

Kathrine Switzer was lured to the mythic destination of the Boston Marathon by her coach Arnie Briggs's many stories. She entered by signing the form, as she always did, K.V. Switzer. She was a true marathon believer and was well trained for the distance. But the fiery Semple saw only someone trying to degrade his beloved race. He chased after Switzer and her Syracuse University teammates and tried clumsily to rip off the offending numbers. A scuffle and shouting ensued, until suddenly Switzer's boyfriend running alongside, a 235-pound hammer thrower and ex-All American footballer, threw a shoulder charge into Semple and sent him flying. By one of those chances that make history, the press vehicle was right alongside. The episode was captured in photographs and eyewitness reports.

Switzer was expelled from the Amateur Athletic Union for, among other crimes, "running with men" and "running without a chaperone." On the long road into Boston that day, she resolved to become a good marathon runner (which she did, with a 2:51), and to create opportunities for women in running (which she also did, organizing many races and the successful Avon international circuit). With other women joining the fight, women officially ran the Boston Marathon in 1972, and had their own Olympic marathon in 1984. They, too, had at last joined the race.

Today, almost half of all marathoners are women. Paula Radcliffe's world record 2:15 would win many races outright, and she is the unquestionable rock star of the sport. Several major marathons now start the elite women's field ahead of the men, giving them genuine competition and prime position for spectators and TV. In just three decades since Jock Semple jumped off the bus, the women have gone from exclusion to exclusivity.

JEAN DRISCOLL seemed the least likely person to undertake the marathon challenge. Born with spina bifida, a devastating neural tube defect which usually results in paralysis, she wore leg braces, and after a series of excruciating surgeries became wheelchair bound. Aching with despair at

Right: Jock Semple attacks Kathrine Switzer for entering the "males only" 1967 Boston Marathon, caught in photos that flashed around the world and ignited the women's running revolution.

how she was depleting her family's financial and emotional resources, Driscoll fell behind in school and was near psychic meltdown when a friend badgered her into playing a game of wheelchair soccer. "The only time I felt really free of my torment was when I was playing sports," she says. "I signed up to participate in every one I could find."

This led to a scholarship at the University of Illinois, where she excelled at basketball and track. Track coach Marty Morse noticed how she enjoyed hard repetitive work, in particular intense 45- to 90-minute sessions on the "rollers" and two-hour outings into relentless prairie winds, sometimes pulling six other wheelchairs on a tow rope. Such dogged persistence led Morse to suggest she try a marathon.

"The marathon is way too long and I thought you had to be crazy to do it," recalls Driscoll. "Finally, to shut up my coach, I did Chicago. My hands were all blistered and bloody and I said to Marty, 'Okay, that's it; I'm never doing this again.' But he said, 'Look! You finished second and qualified for Boston!'" Reluctantly, Driscoll accepted the role of pacing a teammate at Boston. When the teammate moved to the front, Driscoll went right with her.

"Suddenly," Driscoll says, "I was away from her and realized I had a chance of winning. A rush came over me, my emotions went wild, and I pumped my arms with all my might. I saw Finish but didn't let up one bit until I surged across the line. It was a new world record by 7 minutes!

"Once I realized I could do it, there was a fire inside me that wouldn't rest. I wanted to be the best, and I was willing to give it everything I had." In her 15-year career, she won Olympic, Paralympic, and World Championship medals, ranked 25th in *Sports Illustrated for Women*'s Top 100 Female Athletes of the Century, and won eight Boston Marathons—more than any other athlete.

Thanks to athletes such as Driscoll, and the Achilles Track Club, marathons now recognize, among others, people in push-rim wheelchairs and hand-crank cycles, the visually impaired, cancer survivors, amputees, and stroke or MS victims. In a difficult world, the disabled can find unbridled appreciation through the rigors of the marathon.

ONE MORE GROUP has in recent years been joining the race—older runners. Like women, they faced some prejudice in the early days. Peter Foley was excluded from the Boston Marathon for being

Left: Jean Driscoll (second from right) faced discrimination as a handicapped person, but won acclamation as an athlete. Thanks to the pioneering efforts of Bobby Hall in pushing for inclusion of wheelchair racers, Driscoll was able to become one of the greatest marathoners of all time.

too old at age 50, but persisted each year, completing the course for the last time at 85. In the 1970s, as running became a mass health movement as well as a universal sport, the over-40 age groups were a major factor in its growth. Stars emerged, such as Jack Foster, Joyce Smith, Priscilla Welch, Piet van Alphen, and Clive Davies (covering the range from 40 to over-80). Every marathon now has at least an over-40 award category for both sexes, and the better ones recognize 5-year age divisions or offer the level playing field of "age-graded" time adjustment. In 2004, the magazine *More* and the New York Road Runners founded the first marathon for women over 40. The oldest person in every marathon is an instant hero.

Older runners are some of the marathon's most colorful and unlikely characters. Derek Turnbull, the New Zealand sheep farmer who set world records in his sixties, would heave ewes into the pen all week and then put in six-hour runs through mountainous bush at weekends. Ruth Rothfarb, who ran her first marathon at age 81, says she started running at age 72 because "I was tired of all the boring talk about funerals." In 1978, Sister Marion Irvine, a 48-year-old nun, hiding her 198 pounds and her two daily cigarette packs

under a starched white surplice, reluctantly began jogging. Six years later she was the oldest person ever to qualify for a US Olympic trial, was training 85 miles a week in two workouts a day, while still rising before dawn for devotionals and teaching full time. She is almost certainly the only nun to appear on the cover of a national magazine in shorts and singlet.

Kaye Spilker, an art museum curator, ran her first marathon because she was turning 60 and wanted to do something "impossible and outrageous." The marathon is impossible and outrageous. It is also inclusive. It demands no expensive facilities or technical training. It demands only belief, resoluteness, and hard work. It repays those by being heroic, sacred, fulfilling, daunting, and exhilarating. Its appeal is universal, and its participants have become the same. The race is open to anyone who wants to join.

Right: Fauja Singh, here aged 92, after his world age-best 5:40 at the 2003 Scotiabank Toronto Waterfront Marathon, began running at 81 and got his first shoe contract at 90.

11

THE PACK

EVERY MARATHONER RUNS ALONE. Breath, heartbeat, the strike of feet on the road, the sweat-soaked shirt, the aching legs—it's all private. To run the marathon is a wholly personal decision. Only the runner can summon the will to complete it, and the satisfaction of finishing will be each runner's alone.

Yet every marathoner runs with many others— sometimes tens of thousands. They share the road, the purpose, the struggle, and the satisfaction. Together they make up a race, a field, and a community.

In no other endeavor can the ordinary person do the same thing in the same place and at the same time as the best and most famous in the world. Each and every marathoner, however modest in ability or aspiration, can run in the same race as world record holders such as Paul Tergat and Paula Radcliffe. It's like singing at the Met or playing in the US Open. Runners at the back, however far behind the elites, matter just as much. The water stations stay open, the mile clocks keep ticking, and the crowds keep cheering for every runner —and for the whole community of runners.

The marathon attracts people from all walks of life, from all over the world, with every possible kind of motivation. Each has a different story and a different experience in every race. Yet the experience is also shared. Nothing else in the world unites so many people in a single purpose—men and women, rich and poor, from every ethnic group, every age, and in every physical shape.

The marathon running community is a loose but vast collection of individual runners, as well as training groups, teams, clubs, volunteers, coaches, organizers, and just plain friends. At a race, all gather together, milling about the expo, lining up for the pasta party, gathering to hear great runners and speakers. And as the field assembles for the start, they glimpse how huge their community is. All are there to participate, not mere passive spectators.

Busy with the race, very few runners pause to think about the significance of this community or its positive contribution to the world. It is a big claim, but never in human history have so many diverse people combined to participate in such an endeavor, which is wholly healthy, peaceful, and above all active.

Previous spread: The metaphor of "the pack" dates from the days when cross-country running imitated hunting. Like fox hounds, runners still work together and support each other in the long chase, as here at the Scotiabank Toronto Waterfront Marathon.

Right: Runners from at least four continents in the lead pack of the Tokyo International Marathon demonstrate the marathon's global community.

Above: The unprecedented phenomenon of the modern marathon, here waiting to start in the city of Paris.

12

SIDELINES

IF YOU ARE LOSING FAITH in human nature, go and watch a marathon. Tap into the energy of tens of thousands who are out on the streets in the early morning with the sole purpose of urging on people they have never seen before and will likely never see again, yet whose effort they admire and want to encourage. At a marathon you hear none of the partisan tribal boasting and jeering that mar team sports. Onlookers may be watching for one runner—a husband, daughter, friend, grandmother, local hero, village mailman—and they will raise the decibels for any runner whose face or colors they recognize. But they support them all. They want every runner to win, which simply means to finish.

Few of the runners in a marathon are very good at running, but the crowds stay for hours and do their best to help. They are unfailingly generous, benevolent, encouraging, and cheerful, despite the total lack of spectator facilities and information. They have nowhere to sit, no shelter from the weather, no cheerleaders or entertainment. Yet—and it is surely amazing—the citizens of places as diverse as Los Angeles, New York, and Soweto suddenly, one day a year, unite as a community of goodwill, peaceful, patient and positive, without the slightest formal organization or incentive. They simply decide to go out to see the marathon, pick a spot, and squeeze randomly together along the edge of a gutter.

The most famous marathon spectators are the women students of Wellesley College, halfway along the Boston Marathon course. Since early in the 20th century, thousands of exuberant young women have lined the road to cheer the runners past their campus. They clap, skip, smile, beckon, bounce, wave, whoop, and brandish banners that invite you to stop for a hug, and they scream, shriek, squeak, and cheer, cheer, cheer, cheer, until in the middle of their tunnel of energy, by the college gateway, you feel the sound waves physically pound into you like surf. Many male runners live for that moment, though since 1966 the students have given women runners even louder support.

All human celebrations require movement. If the festivity is too big for dancing, people organize parades and processions, and what used to be called a "progress," popping the queen in a coach and trundling her along to the palace. That's why the marathon has become such a distinctive modern form of celebration, the best and biggest folk festival we have. It's mobile and it has meaning. It expresses human energy, effort, movement, courage, and commitment to a challenge. So people watching respond at their best.

It's simple enough, to stand on a marathon course and bang inflated cheer sticks together, or call out numbers to encourage runners you don't know. But in an often troubled and divided world, it is a phenomenon more significant than it looks, and far from fully understood. Do not say the age of miracles is past until you have watched the people watching a marathon.

Previous spread: Spectators at the London Olympic Marathon on July 24, 1908, climb trees for a better view. Marathon day brings out the best in every city, displaying civic pride, neighborliness, tolerance, and enthusiasm for an event that involves everyone.

Above: More than 50 years later, Wellesley College students still line up as these young women did, to support runners at the halfway point of the Boston Marathon.

Above: Thai musicians and children watch the Temple Run. Children are often the most vocal spectators. "Well run!" they cry, or "You can do it!" or *"Allez-allez!"* The most appropriate call is heard on the island of Fiji, where the children simply say "goodbye" as the runners pass.

Above: Spectators cheer at the Jungfrau Marathon, Switzerland. A good view, hands to clap, something to wave... the marathon spectator's needs are very modest, yet the event can make eyes sparkle with delight.

Following spread: Some like to watch in comfort as others do the hard running, evident in the chairs ready for spectators on the sidelines of the Boston Marathon.

Left: Spectators enrich the challenging Jungfrau
Marathon in Switzerland with music.

Above: Orderly schoolgirls add their patient, peaceful,
and positive support to the Coban Marathon, Guatemala.

Above: Some spectators seem impassive. Members of the Jewish community of Brooklyn annually bring their calm gaze to the ING New York City Marathon, among many different ethnic communities who come out along the course.

Right: Other spectators are passionate. Drummers provide rhythm and inspiration for runners on a tough section of the Big Sur Marathon, California.

Left: Vanderlei de Lima of Brazil leads the 2004 Olympic Marathon in Athens. A little later, in a rare incident, he was assaulted by a mentally disturbed onlooker. He recovered and finished third.

Above: Some spectators need not even leave home to get a view of the ING New York City Marathon.

13

HALFWAY

AT THE HALFWAY MARK the marathon runner takes stock. This is done as calmly as possible while running through archways of balloons, past jazz bands, cheering crowds, and past the crucial, all-revealing halfway clock. The halfway mark is the time when many runners perform a check on their condition. How tired are the legs? Is that old injury becoming a problem? Any blisters? Bladder okay? How about the breathing? Any thirst? Body heat? Body heat is an essential consideration. Dumping a cup of water on your head in the middle of the race can be as refreshing as a week's holiday.

The wise runner knows that feeling great at the halfway mark is no guarantee of a good race, but it's the time to identify potential problems. If a brief stop is needed—to visit a restroom or adjust a sock—this is the time to do it, not later when it's harder to regain momentum.

Halfway is the time when the skilled runner begins to concentrate more intently. The first half is for pleasure, enjoying the scenery, the crowds, and the amazing, moving kaleidoscope of runners; it's for thanking the water-station volunteers and relishing the sheer pleasure of moving well. The second half is business. Until now, the runners alongside you have been companions, sharing in a great communal experience. After the halfway mark, especially near the front of the field, they become rivals. The best tactic in the first half is to wait. Now it's time to take charge.

So after the halfway mark is reached, the runner's mind moves more intently inward, attending to the rhythmic footstrike, focusing on smooth movement and maximum pace for minimum expenditure of effort—all the things that come without thought early on but can slip away now. There are always plenty of warning signals around: those runners who are already paying the price for starting too fast, twisting and scowling as they run, slowing to walk, or grabbing cramped thighs, suffering from too much breakfast or too much first-half water. Others give off the opposite signs. It's the strange thing about running: it never feels as fast as it looks when you compare against a fellow runner who is striding so smoothly, running at the same speed as you are.

Halfway is a moment to relish. But a marathon is like a long novel. The first half only sets up the atmosphere and introduces the characters. The real action lies ahead.

Previous spread: Nearly halfway, but many runners find that the mile markers seem to get further apart as the race progresses.

Right: A cup of water is passed to a stranger at the ING New York City Marathon, fulfilling one of the world's oldest gestures of hospitality. Volunteers from local communities enact this ancient ritual at every marathon, often for many hours, for the simple pleasure of making visitors feel welcome.

14

RUN THE WORLD

IN THE FINAL YEARS of the 19th century, no one would have believed that a scattered handful of men struggling to run along a stony road were founding a mass global phenomenon. No one could have imagined how in a little over a hundred years, the marathon would grow, transform, and spread to become an instantly recognized icon.

It first spread thanks to those early races that laid the foundations of its history. These races were run in almost random locations—Boston, Chiswick, Kosice—where enthusiasts eager to foster this strange new pastime found common ground. Then, in the first running boom of the 1970s to 1980s, came the metropolitan marathons, halting the traffic in some of the world's great cities. Now it's hard to name a major city without a marathon.

The human urge to seek new challenges has taken the marathon to courses that are chosen for their exoticism, remoteness, extreme difficulty, natural beauty, and memorable monuments.

These magnificent locales make for a new kind of sport photography—images of runners passing a striking background scene. The background may be a mountain, a cityscape, or a single building. From the North Pole to the Antarctic, from the Swiss Alps to the Sahara Desert, from the streets of Chicago to the temples of Thailand, runners are there, part of international iconography.

What do they mean, these pictures? What do they tell us about our age and our world? With extraordinary vividness, they give us a contemporary vision of humanity's undying impulse to move forward. They speak of challenge, endeavor, determination to achieve, self-sacrifice in a cause, and the joy of pursuing these things in a significant context. Simply put, these marathon images from around the world say a lot about what is great in human society during our time.

Previous spread: Siberian Ice Marathon, Omsk, Russia.

Right: Passing an historic theatre at the LaSalle Bank Chicago Marathon.

Following spread: Kyoto International Marathon, Japan.

Above: Antarctica Marathon, Antarctica.

Right: Runners at the City of Rome Marathon pass the Colosseum.

Following spread: Jungfrau Marathon, Switzerland.

Left: Italian Marathon Memorial Enzo Ferrari, Maranello, Italy.

Above: Despite extreme heat, and, as shown here, occassional sandstorms, the Sahara Marathon in Tindouf, Algeria, is run every year in support of the saharawi refugee camps in the region.

Left: Runners pass historic scenery at the IAAF World Half Marathon Championships in Brussels, Belgium.

Above: Deadwood Mickelson Trail Marathon, South Dakota.

Following spread: The Kilauea Volcano Wilderness Marathon crosses the lava fields of Hawaii Volcanoes National Park on the island of Hawaii.

Left: Blackmores Sydney Marathon, Australia.

Above: The punishing North Pole Marathon was pioneered by race director Richard Donovan, the first marathoner at both the North and South Poles.

Left: Safaricom Marathon, Kenya.

Above: Valencia Marathon, Spain.

Right: Reggae Marathon, Negril, Jamaica.

Left: real-Berlin Marathon, Germany.

Above: Mt. Everest Challenge Marathon, Sandakphu
National Park, Darjeeling, India.

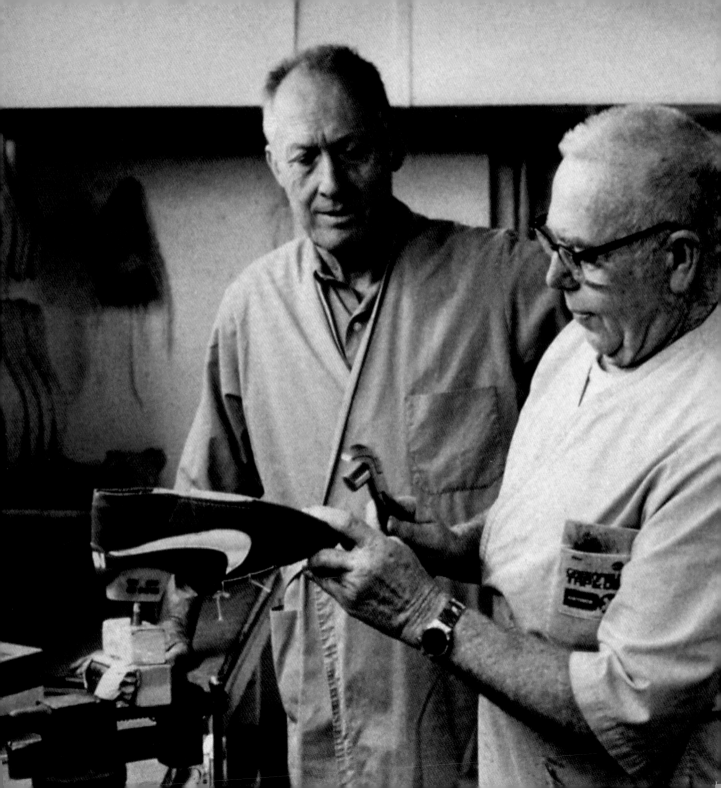

15

GEAR

AHMED SALEH vigorously tapped his chest, *"Je gagnerai! Je gagnerai!"* ("I will win! I will win!"). We were at the practice track two days before the 1988 Olympic marathon in Seoul. The day after he finished third in that race, we met our Djiboutian friend again. Without a word, he flipped off his African sandals to show us a mass of lacerated blisters.

That particular marathon nightmare is much less common than it used to be. In the years of canvas sneakers, stiff leather "pumps," and stony roads, 26 miles turned feet to pulp. Bad shoes changed history, again and again, forcing Johnny Miles out of Boston in 1927, and Johnny Kelley in 1932, years when they should have won.

The marathon imposes hours of relentless repetitive movement. If the moving parts in any machine run less than perfectly, the result is friction. When the machine is the human body, friction means pain. For nearly a hundred years, runners improvised, searching for anything light and friction-free to cover their feet and bodies.

They had to wait until the 1960s for the first lightweight road racing shoes to be invented. Not surprisingly, they were made in Japan, home at that time to many of the world's best runners.

University of Oregon coach, Bill Bowerman, and one of his former athletes, Phil Knight, began to import the Onitsuka company's shoes and sold them in the United States under the name Tiger. While Knight built the business, Bowerman tinkered with the shoes' design. He put nylon uppers on the Tiger composition soles, and the revolutionary Tiger Cortez and Tiger Cub were born. For the first time in a century, many marathoners ran without developing a blister.

In 1971, Knight started to make shoes under the brand Nike, named after the Greek goddess of victory. The company would eventually grow into a $9-billion industry giant. Bowerman kept tinkering. One day he poured rubber into his wife's waffle iron and turned out the mold of a shoe sole covered with miniature studs. Instead of the foot hotly pounding the pavement as it had in the old flat sole, the new sole left cooling air space for the foot as it landed. Since then, most shoe research and technology has focused on that small but critical point of impact—the runner's foot hitting the road. In addition to cushioning choices, runners can now pick shoes that support the foot and counter its tendency to pronate. One 2005 shoe even has a built-in computerized control system

Previous spread: Bill Bowerman (left) was committed to improving the running shoe. He is shown here, with Fred O'Neil, working on an early model.

Right: A pair of well-worn shoes from the 1950s.

that adjusts the response of the sole to every different footstrike.

While early running shoes caused blisters, early running clothing led to chafing. Cotton shorts, shirts, and long pants (for winter training) became stiff with salt and sweat. Always wet with sweat, and often sodden with rain, these clothes were heavy in the summer and dangerously chilling in winter. Their seams were routinely coated in Vaseline to stop chafing, making the clothing dingy to look at and ripe to smell. Bleeding nipples and thighs were commonplace. By the time any garment had been worn to a comfortable flannel-thin softness, it was riddled with holes. It's no wonder that the runners in early marathons are often described as looking like ragged refugees.

The marathon by its very length and severity inflicts demands on clothing well beyond most sports. The first women marathoners found men's shorts and singlets inadequate to accommodate their breasts and rounder hips. Their voices soon joined the men's chorus of complaint about discomfort, chafing, and restricted movement.

It was the 1970s running boom that at last began to solve the problems. Running apparel was transformed by the discovery of lightweight nylon and polyester fibers that wash and dry quickly. Silky, slippery, and chafe-free gear began appearing in the stores. Men and women alike became unabashed about venturing out in close-fitting tights and matching windbreaker jackets.

As innovative as those first polyesters were, today's fabrics were unimaginable only a decade ago. The new featherlight polyesters are not only chafe-free but "breathable," wicking sweat off the body, promoting evaporation, and helping prevent overheating. Other fabrics keep the body warm and allow the transfer of heat and moisture to the outside of the clothing while preventing cold and wind from entering. Runners can now train hard and long in virtually any climate.

The sport's simple fashions—bikini trunks and bra top for women and traditional shorts and singlet for men—leave little room for change. A different color or a shorter hem is about the extent of it. What has changed is what is worn beneath the miracle fabrics. Once the "athletic supporter" was essential male equipment. Supposedly the jockstrap reduced bounce and impact. It also became encrusted with sweat, caused chafing, and promoted crotch fungus, while its broad waistband could inflict side

Left: Loose shorts and sleeveless shirts were state-of-the-art running gear in the early 20th-century.

stitch. It took a lot of nerve for one world-class runner to confess that he ran in his wife's snug nylon underpants, but word soon spread. Now briefs are built into running shorts.

Women likewise were counseled that the bouncing from running would damage their breasts. Although this is another myth, running can indeed be uncomfortable for the well-endowed. While the perfect sports bra is still a work in progress, it has allowed millions of women to run in comfort. Conventional under-wire bras, those instruments of running torture, have joined the jockstrap in the marathon's underwear graveyard.

Today's gear is minimal yet critical. A wrinkled sock can negate years of training, so today's socks are wrinkle-free, wick sweat, and reduce friction. Blister pads and antichafe lubricants guard (if not infallibly) against those old enemies. Knee and ankle supports, arch braces, toe and heel pads, fluid replacement drinks, energy bars, gels, squeeze bottles, and many other products seek to alleviate the discomforts of the marathon or provide fuel. Programmable split-timing wristwatches make possible the finest adjustment to race or training pace, and heart monitors give instant access to the scientific measurement of effort. Enterprising manufacturers have persuaded runners they need to wear caps, glare-reducing sunglasses, compres-sion socks, nose strips, ID tags, wristbands, head-phones, and safari waistbelts, heavily laden with enough water bottles and emergency energy gels to cross the Sahara Desert.

It is ironic, then, that while technology has smoothed the way for new millions to take up marathon running, race performance has declined dramatically since the 1980s, measured in the depth of quality times (for example, the number of sub-3 hours). Has technology made running too comfortable? Has it moved the marathon away from its pure but arduous essence? Has the new gear bred a generation who believe you can buy a better marathon, just as some seek to buy youth-fulness or weight loss? Many runners do indeed go a little faster because modern equipment dimin-ishes those old unpredictable nightmares. But only one thing can lift a runner's performance to a higher level—long-term hard work. No gear can replace that.

Right: Modern runners such as Paula Radcliffe wear the minimum amount of clothing, and benefit from high-tech fabrics and shoes, among other technologi-cal advancements.

Above: In 2005, Adidas released this highly technical shoe with a built-in computerized control system that adjusts the sole to different foot strikes.

Right: Old-time running shoes had soft uppers and thin, frail soles. Blisters were common, but some believe that the simple structure of these shoes made it possible to run naturally—as if barefoot—and caused the foot and ankle to build strength rather than rely on support.

16

RITUAL AND RELIGION

WHEN PHEIDIPPIDES, on his third long day of running, heard his name called by the nature god Pan, it was an encounter of religious significance. Many marathon runners today recognize a similar connection. We do not expect to chat with a goat-footed god, but we do experience the close kinship with nature that Pheidippides's meeting with Pan implies. We do feel a connection between our bodies in motion and our spiritual condition. Our lives have more meaning for the rigorous discipline of our running.

A connection between running and religion is affirmed in many cultures. On Mount Hiei in Japan, Tendai Buddhist monks have long conducted the "moving meditation" of *kaih gy*, running more than 50 miles a day in a 7-year, 1,000-day "Mountain Marathon." In Tibet, too, early explorers record how they met the famous *lung-gom-pa* messenger-monks, running effortlessly all day, apparently in a trance.

The myths and legends of Native Americans often explain the creation of the cosmos and earthly geography in terms of long-distance racing. The Milky Way is the dust raised by a race between the coyote and the wildcat at the beginning of time. Darkness first fell when the sun lost a race against the coyote. The Sacramento River arose as the wake of a runner racing inland.

Christian runners contemplating their sport's connection with spiritual life need look no further than the New Testament letters of St Paul. He repeatedly draws on running and the training it demands as a metaphor for the commitment and rewards of the Christian faith: "Keep yourself in training for religion;" "I run with a clear path before me;" and, in a resonant passage often heard at runners' funerals, "I have run the great race, I have finished my course, I have kept the faith." There was no marathon event in St. Paul's day, but clearly he knew something of the endurance and courage required for distance running.

In our own age, George Sheehan, the runners' guru of the 1970s and 80s, often spoke of the connection. In books such as *Running and Being*, he wrote with a preacher's skill and voice: "I am ready to start a new religion, the first law of which is, 'Play regularly'…heed the inner calling to your own play. Listen if you can to the person you were and can be. Then do what you do best and feel best at."

The spiritual heightening and moral understanding that long-distance running can induce

Previous spread: A peaceful stretch of road at the Big Sur Marathon.

Right: According to Native American belief, the Milky Way is dust raised by runners at the beginning of time.

Running & Being

the total experience

Dr. George Sheehan

has recently been explored in books such as Roger Joslyn's *Running the Spiritual Path* and innumerable personal essays. "Out at mile 25, I feel much closer to God than I ever do in a warm and comfortable church pew," writes William Simpson in *Marathon and Beyond*. "The Talmud uses the metaphor of running in stressing the superiority of Talmud study over ephemeral, worldly pursuits," says Ron Rubin in the *Jewish Journal of Los Angeles*. "The Jew 'runs' towards eternal life, and the marathon runner obeys the Torah's edict 'to watch carefully one's soul.'"

Such thinking was essential to the coaching of Japan's Kiyoshi Nakamura. He inspired great runners such as Toshihiko Seko with teachings from Buddhism, Confucius, the Book of Job, and *The Book of Five Rings* by the Japanese swordsman Miyamoto Musashi. "Anything that contributes to inner growth will benefit performance as a runner," Nakamura said.

Running itself is not a religion, though runners joke about zealous newcomers as "born-again runners." But like religion, it has a spiritual and moral dimension. Like religion, it is a ritual celebrated with a community that also provides intense private fulfillment or consolation. In the days after the horror of September 11, 2001, the running magazines were flooded with contributions by readers who described how their running had enabled them to channel and express their grief. Like some religions, running can also give a sense of oneness with the earth, as it did for Pheidippides and does for the ecstatic marathon monks.

These are the inward, moral, perhaps transcendent effects of long-distance running, an everyday activity that enhances personal lives in ways only too rare in our insecure world.

We know not whom we trust
Nor witherward we fare,
But we run because we must
Through the great wide air.

—Charles H. Sorley, "Song of the Ungirt Runners"

Left: Dr. George Sheehan was a cardiologist, but he could have been a preacher. In resonant, liturgical phrases he prescribed running as a means to better body and soul, and encouraged marathoning as the ultimate pilgrimage of life.

Above, left and right: Many marathoners regularly experience "runner's high," a state of mental elevation during hard exercise, which is induced by endorphins moving through the brain. Runner's high, together with the runner's close contact with the elements and natural terrain, may partly explain the longstanding spiritual or religious dimension to long-distance running. The "moving meditation" rituals of the Tendai Buddhist monks of Mount Hiei in Japan have utilized that connection for many centuries.

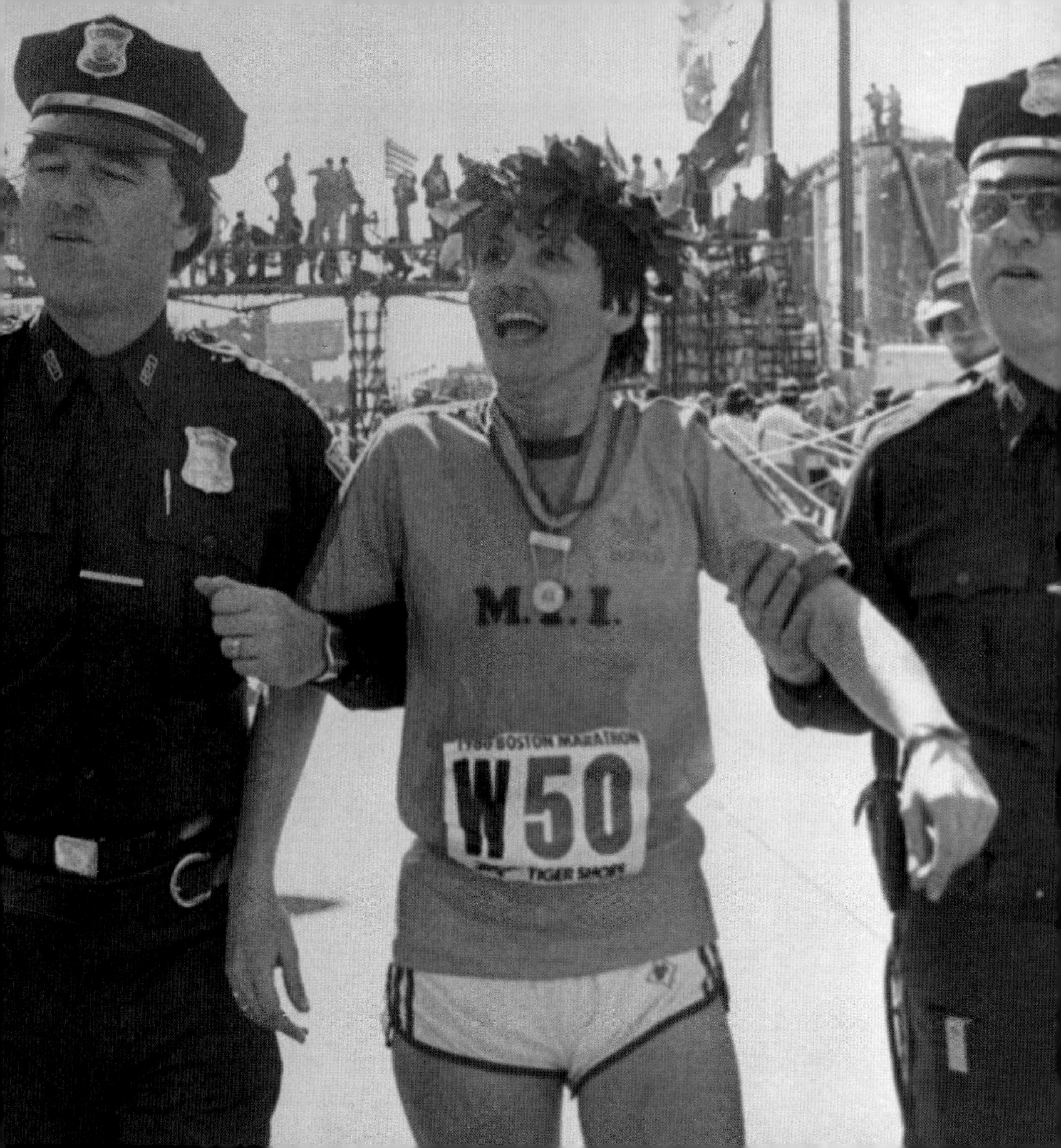
BOSTON MARATHON
W50
TIGER SHOES

17

SHORTCUTS

ON BOSTON MARATHON DAY, near the 25-mile mark on the course, a crowded bar puts up a sign: "Rosie Ruiz starts here." The annual joke has outlasted the famous Rosie T-shirts that showed a New York City subway token, and the fictitious Rosie Ruiz brand of pantihose—"guaranteed not to run." Ruiz left the 1979 New York Marathon in Brooklyn, rode the rest of the course by subway, and came to the finish area, where she was mistakenly scored as a top-ten finisher. She enjoyed the subsequent congratulations so much that she fraudulently cited her New York time to qualify for the Boston Marathon five months later. There she waited among the crowds a mile from the finish, jumped in well ahead of the real women's winner, Canadian Jacqueline Gareau, and exuberantly accepted the laurel wreath. The public thinks the story is funny. Runners think the story is disgraceful. They are still steamed about it, a quarter of a century later.

The self-delusional and unrepentant Ruiz was not the marathon's first cheater, but she has become its most infamous. So much so that the act of cheating in a marathon is called "pulling a Rosie." The first known cheat was in the very first marathon, at the 1896 Athens Olympics, when Spiridon Belokas of Greece claimed third place and the crowd's acclamation. An immediate protest by Gyula Kellner of Hungary led to the revelation that Belokas had ridden some of the later miles in a carriage, alighting in time to run fresh and strong to the finish. He was disqualified.

Perhaps we should not always be harsh. A tired runner can make errors of judgment, especially when the heat of the moment is intensified by the heat of the day. At the 1904 Olympic marathon in St. Louis, humidity and choking dust caused one of the best runners, American Fred Lorz, to drop out at 9 miles. He rode in a newly invented motorcar to 19 miles, where the car broke down. Now rested, Lorz opted to run on instead of waiting for another ride, and found himself passing the race leader and approaching the finish in first place. Famous for his practical jokes, Lorz thought this one was too funny to pass up, so he ran into the stadium to the crowd's applause, and was on the point of accepting the gold medal when the true winner, Thomas Hicks, arrived. Hicks's assistants did not find it funny. Lorz was completely honest about what he had done, but his name even now is associated with that ill-judged joke, despite the fact that he legitimately won the Boston Marathon the next year.

Previous spread: Garlanded in the winner's wreath and medal at Boston, 1980, the noticeably sweat-free Rosie Ruiz enjoys the traditional police escort to the press conference, where she was quickly discovered to be a fraud.

Right: After a week of investigation, Canadian Jacqueline Gareau was declared the rightful women's winner, and a victory ceremony with men's winner Bill Rodgers was re-enacted. But the cheering crowds had long gone; nothing could restore the moment of hard-earned triumph that Ruiz had stolen.

Others have cheated in much more calculating ways. One man claimed masters' over-50 victories in the 1978 New York City and 1979 Boston marathons by slipping into the fields mid-way, but was foolish enough to claim a time at Boston that supposedly broke the world age-group record. Another who cheated his way to a masters' award proved to be a wealthy businessman, who had flown from California to run only the last miles of the New York City Marathon. There are also several cases of people accepting age-group awards after passing their bib numbers to younger runners.

What compels these people to cheat? The monetary rewards are trivial. There was no prize money at Boston until six years after Rosie. It seems that the fantasy of being a sporting success overrides judgment, decency, and any sense of the rights of the true winners. Acclamation from the crowds and praise from friends are powerfully seductive. The dream appears to be particularly compelling to middle-aged men who have been successful in other fields. Their mindset seems similar to those who for centuries have falsely claimed to be war heroes, but it bewilders true runners, whose objective is to finish the course—first beat the distance, then beat your best time, and then, if possible, the

opposition. How can you cry "Rejoice, we conquer," when you know you haven't conquered?

Such cheaters also infuriate runners, who see them as deviants who deprive the real winners of their place in history—a small place, indeed, but significant to those who have worked so hard to achieve it. For Jacqueline Gareau, the rightful Boston winner in 1980, it was a nightmare to be deprived of her triumphal moment, breaking the tape in a glorious course record. To win like that is the hope or fantasy that sustains elites and joggers alike through thousands of lonely training miles.

Annoying as they are, shortcutters have forced marathon organizers to make changes that have improved the sport. Before Rosie, even major marathons such as Boston were often poorly organized, and treated women and the over-40 age groups as merely part of the pack. After Rosie, with professionalism also soon raising the stakes, careful surveillance began to record and acknowledge all runners. Close marshalling of the course to exclude cheats required hundreds of new race workers, but also increased course safety and crowd control. Where video surveillance was used, it could provide runners with individual video souvenirs.

Right: This Boston newspaper headline trumpets Fred Lorz's win, a year after his practical joke finish at the Olympics.

In 1993, the ChampionChip system provided a technological breakthrough that eliminated cheaters by recording intermediate and finish times for every runner. No one can dodge the system's magic-carpet scrutiny.

Unfortunately, no technological device yet exists to stop those "bandits" who gatecrash races, cluttering the road and freeloading off the entry fees that every other runner has paid. Some races now use corral systems to control another irritating group, the overconfident runners who line up to start at mile-pace marks well ahead of their capability, and create a risky and frustrating situation for the better runners behind them.

Much more consequential, threatening indeed the whole sport at elite level, is drug cheating. Slick so-called athletes, enticed by prize and endorsement money and often supported by medical crews, enhance their performances artificially despite all attempts to control the problem by legislation. There has been one high-profile Olympic disqualification for banned drugs, when Madina Biktagirova was disqualified after placing fourth in the 1992 Olympic marathon. Two gold medals, in 1976 and 1980 by Waldemar Cierpinski, are now known to have been gained with the help of banned steroids administered by the East German regime. Silver medallists Frank Shorter and Gerhardus Nijboer might justly feel as aggrieved as Gyula Kellner did when Belokas jumped out of his carriage in 1896.

The gravity of this particular shortcut goes deeper than depriving rightful athletes of the achievement and financial rewards they have earned. It robs the whole sport of its purity. Every time we doubt a runner's improvement, every time an outstanding performance makes us pause before we applaud, a great sport dies a little. We need to believe in those we admire. And we need to be able to recommend the marathon to our children and friends, as a sport that rewards the honest effort of covering the whole course.

Left: Despite eyewitness accounts of her jumping in the race at mile 25 and her own inability to answer questions about the race and her training, Ruiz tearfully maintained her innocence and has refused to this day to return the champion's medal.

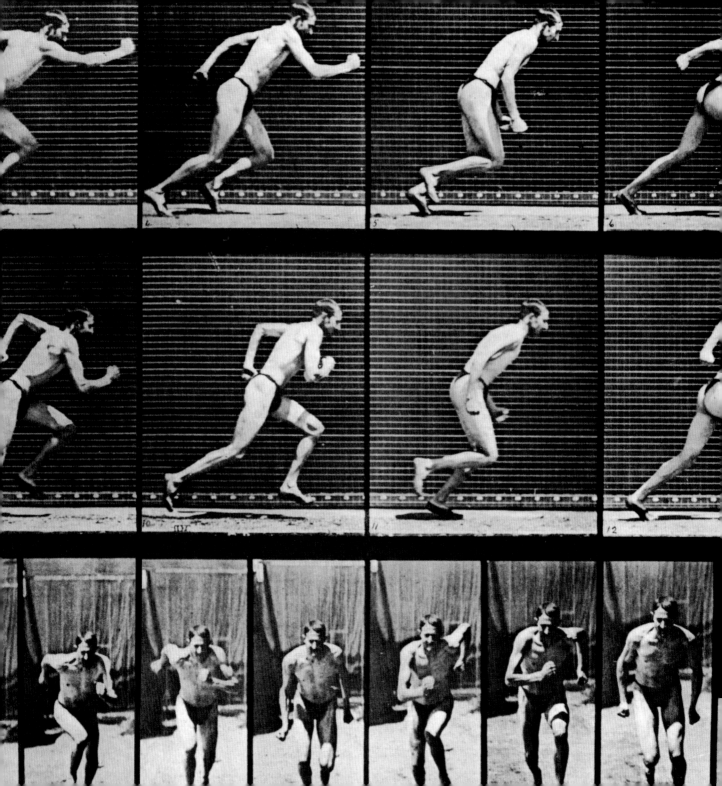

18

THE BODY IN QUESTION

26 MILES OF RUNNING mean 50,000 strides propelling the body against gravity and air resistance; 50,000 footstrikes on an unyielding road; 25,000 heartbeats, pumping 4,000 liters of blood that carry crucial oxygen to the working muscles at the outer extremities of the body; more than 10 pounds of water exuded through sweat; 3,000 calories burned; the body's stored energy virtually depleted. The figures are approximate—ballpark estimates for a 150-pound male running 3:30—but very impressive. Running a marathon is demanding work for the body. When Hamlet spoke of the thousand natural shocks that flesh is heir to, he was several thousand short for the average marathon.

Every marathon performance is determined by the runner's innate genetic makeup, training, prior hydration and nutrition, preparation of footwear and apparel, the day's conditions, immediate health, pace judgment, mental application—and luck. Many a fine marathon has ended at an unseen pothole or in an accidental tangle with another runner. The body needs to be in perfect order for a marathon, not battered and bleeding.

Genetics decide the proportion of slow-twitch muscle fibers that are required for a marathon-apt body. Training adapts the body for every other need. The key ones are glycogen storage, fat utilization, maximal oxygen uptake, efficient processing of oxygen at race pace, and high lactate threshold. The most obvious limiting factor is energy storage. Enough glycogen/carbohydrate is stored in the muscles and liver to last most runners about 20 miles. Since the distance between Marathon and Athens is more than that, supplies are often expended. Then the body has to switch to its long-term fat reserves, which can be slow to come into operation.

The marathon's one-time reputation as damaging and dangerous is happily a thing of the past. Runners still get tired, and limp about with sore calf muscles and battered feet for days after the race. The physical challenge is no less than it ever was. But we are so much better trained, we know so much more, we take precautions against so many marathon ailments, that the long-term benefits for the body now far outweigh the discomforts. More efficient use of energy and oxygen, and better processing of blood to the muscles and brain, are benefits that last longer than 26.2 miles. The body in shape for a marathon is a body in shape for life.

Previous spread: Eadweard Muybridge's famous stop-frame photos from *Animal Locomotion* (1887) depicted the perfect human animal at full speed.

Right: Just as wounded animals wade in cold streams, some runners believe that an ice bath after a marathon can aid recovery by stopping the swelling and bleeding from millions of tiny muscle tears.

THE BODY IN QUESTION

1. Brain: Some sports psychologists claim that 60 to 90 percent of success is due to "psychological mastery," which is why techniques such as visualization may help runners override awareness of tiredness and pain.

2. Heart: The optimal heart rate for most marathoners is 70 percent of the individual's maximum heart rate (MHR), though elites are trained to sustain higher levels. Marathon training and racing elevate HDL ("good cholesterol") in the blood, greatly reducing the risk of heart disease.

3. Nipples: As the most prominent and sensitive area on the chest, they are highly vulnerable to painful abrasions, even bleeding, from sweat and salt-encrusted shirts, and garment seams diabolically sewn across the nipples.

4. Sweat glands: The sweating process is less efficient in hot, humid weather when it becomes harder to transmit heat into the air. Lack of sufficient fluids causes decreased blood volume and dehydration, which can eventually cause overheating and heat exhaustion or heatstroke (hyperthermia). However, excess hydration may dangerously dilute the blood's sodium level (hyponatremia). Both can be deadly.

5. Arms: The arms are a common location for tension, causing tight running form and eventually fatigue. Strong arms help carry themselves over long distances.

6. Hands: They are best held loose, not clenched tight, as this causes tension. Hands are the most vulnerable body part in a cold-weather marathon because of the windchill effect from movement through cold air and lack of fat over the wrist pulse point.

7. Diaphragm: This is the location of "side stitch," a spasm, cramp, or, if persistent, bruising of the diaphragm muscles. Causes of this common discomfort include inadequate training, uneven gait, starting too fast, and undigested food blocking blood flow and thus oxygen to the area.

8. Liver: The liver converts carbohydrate from food into glycogen, the source of marathon power. A good pre-marathon storage level is 2,000 calories. This supplies 75 to 90 percent of energy in the early miles. When glycogen stores dwindle at about 20 miles, depending on effort, the body switches to burning mainly stored fat. However, there is a lag before fat burning takes over, marked by heavy legs, diminished coordination, and mental fuzziness. This point is called "the wall" because it feels like suddenly running into one.

9. Stomach: Blood necessary for marathoners' muscles will be uncomfortably directed to digesting food unless the pre-race meal is eaten at least two hours before the race.

10. Fat: Because fat is weight to carry, each 1 percent reduction in body fat can represent a 1 percent improvement in performance. But even thin runners carry 8 or more important pounds in storage. Late in a marathon, the fatty acids in this stored fuel get burned, with each pound supplying 3,500 calories of energy.

11. Bladder: Properly hydrated runners' urine should be pale yellow. Dark urine usually indicates dehydration. Brown urine or blood in urine (runner's hematuria) is usually the result of severe dehydration, which irritates bladder walls.

12. Skeleton: The ideal marathoner's structure is ectomorphic—light and narrow-framed. The density and strength of all weight-bearing bones are greatly increased by regular running, provided adequate nutritional and hormonal levels are maintained.

13. Muscle fibers: Good marathon runners generally have a preponderance (75 percent) of "slow twitch" fibers that work a long time without tiring. (Sprinters have more "fast twitch" fibers; the average population has 50 percent of each.) Within a muscle's mitochondria, oxygen burns glycogen to create energy. However, a muscle's ability to use the oxygen it receives is affected by lactate, a by-product of burning carbohydrate that overaccumulates during a marathon, causing a stinging sensation in muscles. Each runner's lactate threshold is a major limiting factor in marathon performance, but this can be raised by training.

14. Quadriceps muscles: Good marathon runners usually stride relatively short and low, because overstriding uses too much energy for the ground gained, and striding high fights gravity and increases impact on landing.

15. Knee: The location of 60 percent of running injuries, it is designed to move in one plane—forward. If it wobbles sideways, when the foot overpronates, or twists from a sideways motion coming up from a weak arch or ankle, after 25,000 lateral wobbles it will be sorely tested.

16. Feet: Each running foot strikes the road and propels the body upward and forward about 90 times a minute. Multiplied by 25,000 times over the course of a marathon, small problems can become large ones. It is common for toenails to blacken and fall off after a race.

MARATHON

PRODUCTS

"BEST IN THE LONG RUN"
REG. U.S PAT OFF

19

THE STORY OF A WORD

And Marathon became a magic word.
— George Gordon, Lord Byron,
"Childe Harold's Pilgrimage"

UNTIL 1896, THE NAME Marathon evoked the victory of freedom. New towns were called Marathon in Ontario, Florida, Iowa, New York, Texas, and Wisconsin, the name paying tribute to Greece, freedom, and democracy.

Then Spiridon Louis ran from Marathon to Athens and the word took on new meanings.

Thanks to Louis's famous 1896 home victory, the phrase "marathon race" entered the world's vocabulary, soon simplified to "marathon." The word denoted the new long-distance event, and also conjured up long and heroic effort. When Dorando Pietri staggered and fell in front of 100,000 spectators in London in 1908, the word also took on the meanings of struggling against exhaustion, endurance tested to the point of breakdown. Only four months later, the new word was applied outside running, when an English newspaper reported a "Murphy's Marathon," a contest to peel 25 pounds of potatoes.

"Marathon mania," as it was called, swept the world after the Pietri drama. In New York, Buffalo and elsewhere, the celebrities of the London Olympic race—Pietri, Johnny Hayes, and Canadian Tom Longboat—were matched and re-matched, against each other and new marathoners including English track-record holder Alfred Shrubb and Frenchman Henri St Yves. They raced marathons for prize money, around and around tiny tracks in front of huge high-betting crowds. In one fetid indoor arena, Shrubb choked on the dense tobacco smoke. Many new road marathons under amateur rules were also created. The official report on the London Olympics scornfully dismissed all this as an "epidemic of 'Marathon Races' which attacked the civilized world." Like it or not, suddenly everyone had heard of the marathon.

The word made its first literary appearance in *The History of Mr. Polly*, a comic novel by H.G. Wells, written in London during 1909, with the Pietri race still fresh. A foul-mouthed criminal, Uncle Jim, appears alongside Mr. Polly as he is out walking and warns him to "scoot."

"Mr. Polly…quickened his pace.

'Arf a mo', said Uncle Jim, taking his arm. 'We ain't doing a (sanguinary) Marathon. It ain't a (decorated) cinder track. I want a word with

Previous spread: A replica of a 1940s gas pump decal advertises Marathon Petroleum.

Right: After Dorando Pietri's dramatic collapse at the 1908 Olympics "marathon mania" ignited into a hugely popular sport. Rivalry between Pietri and gold medalist Johnny Hayes became the perfect lure for spectators hoping to witness more suffering or anxious to bet on the outcome.

you, mister. See?'"

At the same time, a young composer in the United States wrote a comic song called "Dorando," about the new sport. It is not the tribute to Pietri that almost everyone has assumed. An Italian New Yorker laments, in stage-Italian English, that he sold his barbershop to bet on Pietri in a Madison Square Garden marathon ("One-a, two-a hundred times around da ring") and lost his money when Pietri gave up ("Dorando he's a drop!"). The songwriter was Isador Baline, later known as Irving Berlin.

"Marathon" had arrived, not only as the name of a new sport with unique popular appeal, but as a word that usefully connotes endurance or excess. The word took on new linguistic life in the 1920s with the American Depression craze for "dance marathons." From then on, its figurative uses have been endless—marathon political debates, marathon law cases, marathon theater festivals, marathon love affairs.

Businesses and charities were quick to seize on the positive associations of long-lasting endurance or energy, or in recent years, good health. Marathon has become the name of an oil company, electric generator, fuel cell, water heater, film producer, boat and canoe manufacturer, sports-goods catalog, disaster tolerance service, computer network service, chocolate candy bar, and rubber farm boot. In the late 1950s the word was broken in half, and "-thon" or "-athon" was used as a suffix, often applied to fund-raising efforts. So there were—and still are—walkathons, telethons, moviethons, pianothons, and many more.

Any sport testing endurance is likely now to be called a marathon, whatever its distance. There are current examples from swimming to sled-dog racing. But marathon running is bigger, more vigorous, and more universal. When a movie is released with a title such as *Marathon Man* (the Dustin Hoffman/Laurence Olivier thriller), no one expects it to be about a potato-peeling contest. The word "marathon" has become deeply established as a metaphor, but the marathon itself is in no danger of surrendering its name.

Left: Soon "marathon" meant anything long-lasting or showing long-term resilience. Here couples in a 1928 dance marathon in Culver City, California, step and twirl 8 miles down the highway to Ocean Park.

Marathon™

ENERGY SAVER MINI DECORATIVE TWISTER

LASTS 7 YEARS† GUARANTEED
See side panel for details††

SAVE $45 IN ENERGY COSTS

MARATHON®
The Long Distance Runner™

7 1/4" (184 mm)

Max RPM 8,300
5/8" (16 mm) Arbor / Eje / Mandrin

FOR WOOD CUTTING USE ONLY
SOLAMENTE PARA
CORTAR MADERA
CONÇUES UNIQUEMENT
POUR COUPER LE BOIS

See power tool owner's manual for proper use.
Consulte el manual del propietario de la herramienta
mecánica para verificar el uso apropiado.
Consulter le manuel du propriétaire de cet outil électrique
pour s'assurer de sa bonne utilisation.

MARATHON®
IRWIN®
24030

24T
Framing/
Ripping

Enmarcar/
tronzar
Charpenterie/
sciage en
long

IRWIN®

Hecho en Japón
Fabriqué au Japon

MARATHON®
BY Lincoln®
Professional Cookware

GAMMA®

Extra Durable
Diamond Pearl Coating

Marathon™ DPC 15L
Diamond Pearl Coating Provides Extra Durability for Hard Hitters

ADVANCED
agp
Gamma Processing

15L Ga
1.40
40 F
12.2 Met

Left: Many products benefit from the connotation of excellence and endurance that the word "marathon" imparts. Clockwise from top left: Phillips lightbulb; Irwin Tools saw blade; Pro Penn tennis balls; Goodyear tire; Gamma tennis racquet strings; Lincoln Foodservice Products stockpot.

20

HEROES 1956–1982

Jim Peters England, b. 1918
Best time: 2:17:40 (1954)

The London railworker's son revolutionized the marathon, hacking 8 minutes from the world record. First to break 2:20, he won seven major marathons, four of them in world records. He collapsed from dehydrated exhaustion in the hot 1954 Empire Games, and never ran again.

Emil Zatopek Czechoslovakia, b. 1922
Best time: 2:23:04 (1956)

The most inspirational runner in history, Zatopek won only one marathon, the 1952 Olympic race, but it gave him sporting immortality and a unique treble of Olympic victories. He is still revered for his innovatively hard training and his unfailing personal kindness.

Sergey Popov USSR, b. 1930
Best time: 2:15:17 (1958)

The Asian Russian from eastern Siberia pillaged the 1958 European championship and the world record, both by more than 2 minutes. His times led the world 1957–1959. Favorite for the 1960 Olympics, he was surprised by Bikila, and finished fifth, but still placed well in major races until 1963.

Dale Greig Scotland, b. 1937
Best time: 3:27:45 (1964)

The Scot ran the first fully authenticated marathon by a woman, May 23, 1964, in the notoriously hilly Isle of Wight Marathon. She was four times Scottish cross-country champion (1960–1968) and set a women's record in the London-Brighton run. Competed to 1987, and still serves as administrator.

Buddy Edelen United States, b. 1937
Best time: 2:14:28 (1963)

A track runner, he moved to England as a teacher, where 135 miles weekly hardened him into the world's best marathoner. First American to break 2:20, he won three major marathons in 1963, and in 1964 set a world record winning the revered Polytechnic. Sciatica ended his Olympic hopes.

Abebe Bikila Ethiopia, b. 1932
Best time: 2:12:12 (1964)

Twice won the Olympics in a world record, sport's ultimate achievement. Unknown in 1960, he glided barefoot through Rome's dark streets, and with equal serenity broke the record by nearly 2 minutes in 1968. Won 10 other major marathons, but was paralyzed in a 1969 car crash.

Basil Heatley England, b. 1933
Best time: 2:13:55 (1964)

Moving to the marathon after success in cross-country and track, Heatley won the 1964 Polytechnic, in a world record 2:13:55. At the Tokyo Olympics, he carved through the top places, entered the stadium third, and unleashed a merciless finish past Kokichi Tsubaraya for the silver.

Brian Kilby England, b. 1938
Best time: 2:14:43 (1963)

In 10 months from 1962–1963, he won the European and Commonwealth titles, placed third at Boston (beating Bikila), and ran the world's second fastest time, missing Edelen's new world record by 15 seconds. At the 1964 Olympics, he ran tactically with Coventry clubmate Heatley, and finished fourth.

Kenji Kimihara Japan, b. 1941
Best time: 2:13:33.4 (1967)

Japan in the 1960s claimed more than half the world's top 10 marathon times each year. Kimihara stands out for his high-level consistency, including eighth, second, and fifth in three Olympics. He also compiled international victories including the Asian Games, Boston, Beppu, and Polytechnic.

Morio Shigematsu Japan, b. 1940
Best time: 2:12:00 (1965)

In a meteoric four-month rise in 1965, he placed fourth at Beppu in February, destroyed a top field and the course record at Boston in April, and set an inspired world record, winning the Polytechnic by 2 minutes in June. The comet then fell, and the business studies graduate never broke 2:16 again.

Derek Clayton Australia (b. England), b. 1942
Best time: 2:08:34 (1969)

His two world records were far ahead of their time, like his intensive training. At Fukuoka in 1967, he slashed off nearly 3 minutes, with 2:09:36.4, then cut that to 2:08:33.6 at Antwerp. Injuries left the unchallenged leader of his era with no Olympic medal.

Mamo Wolde Ethiopia, b. 1932
Best time: 2:15:08.4 (1972)

Emerging from Bikila's shadow in 1968 in the altitude of Mexico City, he took the 10,000-meter silver, and dominated the marathon by 3 minutes. Ran 5 minutes faster for third at the 1972 Olympics, his personal best at age 40. Died of illness exacerbated by prolonged political imprisonment.

Bill Adcocks England, b. 1941
Best time: 2:10:47.8 (1968)

Over the hot Marathon to Athens hills, the gritty Adcocks won a 1969 rematch of the Olympic top 5 by 2 minutes. His 2:11:07.2 course record lasted until the 2004 Olympics, on much-improved road surfaces. In 1968, he set a European record and won Fukuoka in a superlative 2:10:47.8.

Ron Hill England, b. 1938
Best time: 2:09:28 (1970)

His long career peaked in 1969–1970, when he won the European championship, was second in Fukuoka, won Boston in a course record, and won the Edinburgh Commonwealth Games in 2:09:28, the world's second best time. Also celebrated for his "streak" of running daily since 1964.

Frank Shorter United States, b. 1947
Best time: 2:10:30 (1972)

He had a perfect flowing stride and almost perfect record—gold and silver Olympic medals, Pan American Games victory, four wins at Fukuoka (1971–1974), and second at New York (1976). A lawyer, commentator, and founder of a line of running apparel, he also chaired the US anti-doping agency.

Ian Thompson England, b. 1949
Best time: 2:09:12 (1974)

Like the hero of a schoolboy story, the unknown club runner captured the 1973 English title in history's fastest debut time (2:12:40). He dominated the 1974 Commonwealth marathon, his 2:09.12 within sight of Clayton's world record, and did it again in the European championship in the heat of Rome.

Jack Foster New Zealand (b. England), b. 1932
Best time: 2:11:18.8 (1974)

Inspiration of the masters movement, he ran for the first time at 32. At 39, he placed third at Fukuoka, at 40, eighth in the 1972 Olympics, and at 41, second in the Common-wealth Games. His best time lasted 16 years as world masters record. Ran 2:20:28 at 50.

Michiko Gorman United States (b. China to Japanese parents), b. 1935
Best time: 2:39:11 (1976)

The tiny Japanese-American linked up in Los Angeles with the great coach Laszlo Tabori and redefined American women's running with her 2:46:36 in 1973. She then rewrote standards for older women, winning Boston at 38, and after 40 won Boston again and New York twice.

Jerome Drayton Canada (b. Germany), b. 1945
Best time: 2:10:08.4 (1975)

Fearlessly aggressive, he won Fukuoka three times and Boston in 1977. Second at New York in 1977 and the 1978 Commonwealth Games, he was sixth at the 1976 Olympics. His 2:11:13 in 1969 was then third fastest all-time.

Jacqueline Hansen United States, b. 1948
Best time: 2:38:19 (1975)

The first woman in the world to run faster than 2:45 and 2:40, she won at Culver City (three times), Boston, Eugene, Honolulu, and Weott. She was a leading activist for women's distance running, especially in the campaign for Olympic inclusion.

Chantal Langlace France, b. 1955
Best time: 2:35:15.4 (1977)

Despite official discouragement (she was once disqualified because her top was not tucked into her shorts), she traveled to Ernst van Aaken's inaugural women's marathon at Waldniel in 1974. She twice set the world record (1974, 1977), and competed often in the seminal Avon women's circuit.

Christa Vahlensieck Germany, b. 1949
Best time: 2:34:47.5 (1977)

Won the first women's championship, at Waldniel in 1973, and van Aaken's second international women's marathon. Second at Boston in 1974, she twice set the world record (1975, 1977). Favorite to win New York in 1978, she witnessed the new era when Grete Waitz glided past.

Bill Rodgers United States, b. 1947
Best time: 2:09:27 (1979)

An American icon, he won Boston four times (1975, 1978–1980), New York four times (1976–1979) and Kyoto, Amsterdam, and Fukuoka (all 1977). His unfailing affability belies his racing focus and sustained tenacity, and he has competed as an age-group elite for an unequaled 31 years.

Joyce Smith England, b. 1937
Best time: 2:29:43 (1982)

The marathon came late for Smith, a track and cross-country international for 22 years before running her first in 1979, age 41. She won Avon, Tokyo twice, and the new London Marathon twice, including her best time at age 44. In 1984, she ran 2:32:48 as an inaugural Olympian at age 46.

21

THE COURSE AND THE CAUSE

THE MARATHON, all runners will agree, carries meanings greater than an ordinary race. Most runners today are in a marathon not only to race well or improve their health, but for some larger and more selfless purpose—to raise money for a charity, honor a dead parent or friend, or support a cause.

Why does the marathon have this extra dimension?

In part, it comes from the elemental simplicity of long-distance running and its connection over the centuries with spiritual life. In its earliest origins, competitive running was part of the funeral rituals of Bronze Age Myceneans and the creation ceremonies of Native Americans. The ancient Greeks held games to worship their gods and honor dead heroes—just as today's runners often dedicate a marathon in commemoration, privately or in groups such as Fred's Team, honoring former New York Marathon director Fred Lebow, and funding research into brain cancer, the disease that killed him.

In part, it comes from the marathon's difficulty, its image as the ultimate challenge. Such a long race demands qualities that we universally admire—determination, courage, and speed. Body and spirit must work together, and the marathon can symbolize that harmony.

And in part, running a marathon can be a way of affirming our commitment to a cause, because it is the most public of sports. It is played out on the streets, not in a stadium or a pool. It is an individual challenge, yet can involve the whole community. Urban marathons communally celebrate the city that hosts them, rural marathons the value of the natural environment.

So marathons often become symbols of freedom, peace, health, or some other ideal. The first marathon testified to Greece's courageous resilience after centuries of oppression. In 1924, with the shadow of World War I still present, the Czech town of Kosice founded the Peace Marathon. In 1990, when the Berlin Wall fell, that city's race became known as the Run Free Marathon. In the weeks after 9/11, the Marine Corps Marathon in Washington, DC, and the New York City Marathon affirmed more movingly thsan many other events the resolve of those cities to return to business as usual—especially to the peaceful communal celebration that a marathon essentially is.

It was in the 1960s that "runathons," and other endurance "-athons" of all kinds, became widespread as a way of raising money for charities. Then in 1980, Terry Fox, a young Canadian from British Columbia, who had lost a leg to cancer, decided to defy the inevitable and go running. He set out from St John's, Newfoundland, on an extraordinary Marathon of Hope, running a marathon a day across that vast country, raising money for cancer research.

With his one leg and one prosthesis, Fox ran

Previous spread: Terry Fox is the epitome of running for a cause. Although he died before his trans-Canada Marathon of Hope was completed, his heroic legacy continues to grow, inspire, and raise millions of dollars for cancer research.

Right: Running embodies freedom of movement, and the 1990 Berlin Marathon, which crossed into the once-forbidden east after the Berlin Wall fell, became the emotional symbol of reunified Europe. Western competitors donated money to enable impoverished runners from former Communist states to take part.

more than 3,000 miles before the spreading cancer forced him to stop in Thunder Bay, Ontario. In reality he has never stopped. His run inspired a nation. He single-handedly raised $20 million, and the Terry Fox Foundation has since contributed hundreds of millions to cancer research. Twenty-five years after his death at age 22, Terry Fox is a revered Canadian icon—because he ran a course for a cause.

The next major step in the association of marathons with charity was the creation of the London Marathon and the London Marathon Charitable Trust in 1981. One of the race's six objectives was "to raise money for the provision of recreational facilities to London." It was an inspired move. Professionalism was about to become part of marathon running, with all its potential for public resentment about streets being closed and civic services used for money-winning runners. The London Marathon's charitable purpose diverted criticism and drew a huge wave of support to the event. Contributing £36 million a year to more than 700 charities, donating £2 million to London's recreation facilities, in 25 years it has raised the equivalent of over half a billion US dollars.

The value of this philanthropy is beyond question, although doubts have been raised about the long-term effects if marathon running becomes dependent on charities for public legitimacy. London and other high-profile marathons reserve large numbers of race entries for charities, which pay rates well above the conventional entry fees. The charities allocate these entries to money-raising donors, some of whom stroll through the course once and never return, while many long-term committed runners are excluded.

Significantly, some marathons now insist that their prime cause is the marathon itself, and the health and lifestyle benefits it provides.

In a positive-minded sport, charities have become a valued part of the potent mix that makes the modern marathon so universal in its appeal. Like the global stars flying along out front, and the competitive runners behind them, and the health-seeking joggers behind them, the charity runners bring their own purpose and find their own fulfillment. In their purple Team In Training uniforms or chicken outfits or deep-sea diving suits (like the famous participant at London who took 7 days to finish, wearing lead boots), they add variety, color, and, above all, a sense of mission and benevolence. They help the marathon to be much more than 26.2 miles.

Left: U.S. Army veteran Mike Bowen began running in 1984, to help overcome weight, alcohol, and tobacco problems, and to pay tribute to lost buddies. Dedicating each mile run to an American killed or missing in action in Vietnam has kept his passion strong. He's completed 35,000 miles of the 58,196 that is his goal.

Left: These Leukemia & Lymphoma Society's Team In Training runners proudly wear their signature purple shirts. Since 1988 volunteer participants in the program have dedicated their marathons to the cause and raised over $595 million.

Above: The marathon recalls a military victory, but has became a metaphor for peace, whether it's the Kosice Peace Marathon in Slovakia, Tegla Loroupe's Peace Foundation Runs in Kenya, or this "peace" flag flying in Rome.

22

THE AGONY

MANY BOOKS AND ARTICLES have explained what causes "the wall"—that lag time before energy from burning stored fat becomes available after the body's glycogen stocks have been depleted. We know, too, what it looks like when a marathoner hits the wall—those sad, familiar images of Dorando Pietri collapsing for the fourth time on the White City track in 1908, or Jim Peters staggering helplessly on sagging, rubbery legs from side to side at Vancouver in 1954, or the many friends and fellow runners who suddenly slump to a shuffling walk somewhere after 18 miles. Even world-ranked runners drift off the back of the lead pack with that bewildered, slightly glazed expression we all recognize so well.

But what does it feel like? It was an unknown English marathoner in the early 1970s who came up with the colorful description that it felt like hitting a wall. "Hitting the wall" became a familiar colloquial metaphor among England's serious competitive runners, but in 1980 the phrase was still unknown outside their small circle. One innocent and literal-minded British newspaper reporter, having heard Bernie Ford use the phrase to describe his disappointing race in the Moscow Olympic marathon, wrote "Ford became so tired that he veered off the course and bumped into a wall." Fifteen years later, when the marathon had turned into a mass popular phenomenon, the phrase had made its way to North America and all runners knew what hitting the wall meant.

It happens so suddenly that it truly feels like colliding with an unseen barrier. It's like falling into a deep pit, and every step from that moment seems uphill. A kind of gray pain spreads from the legs up, until the whole body stings and aches and becomes enfeebled. There is a mutiny of the legs—they stop running on their own accord. Without any conscious decision, the runner is suddenly walking. Only extreme mental effort will force the legs back into a shuffling jog—but then they stop and walk again.

Emotional reactions often include despair, a profound disillusionment with the whole idea of running a marathon, and short-fused irritation with other people. Every marathoner who has ever hit the wall describes how he or she began to react negatively to the spectators. They didn't want to be encouraged; they wanted to suffer alone. "No, I can't do it," they grumbled inwardly. "And I'm not looking good."

All they want to do is stop. Those that do regret it. For those who struggle through this patch, keep plodding along, fueled by the deep purpose engrained in months of training, better things may lie ahead. Fat stores may kick in (there are no guarantees, but usually there is some improvement). The feeling returns that the marathon is worth the extreme effort it takes. The race is there to be finished, after all. The legs keep running, however slowly. Even the crowd's urgings can begin to seem welcome again. "Just maybe," the runner thinks as the dark fog of despair lifts, "maybe I can do it."

Previous spread: A runner at the Boston Marathon is just able to crawl across the finish line after hitting the wall.

Right: Not all tears at a marathon are tears of joy—sometimes the struggle is too much.

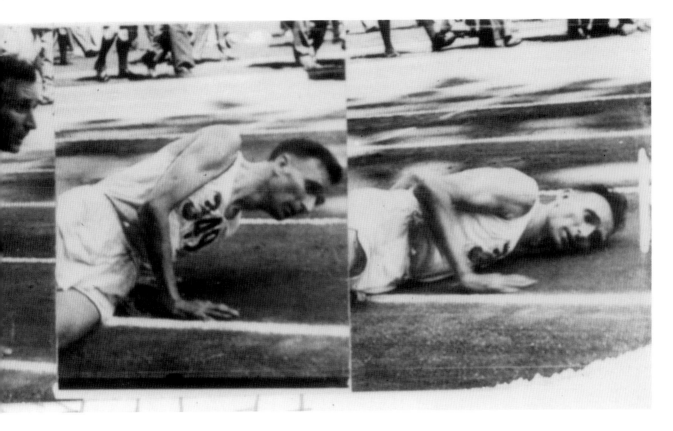

Above: World record holder Jim Peters of England suffered heat exhaustion in the 1954 Empire Games marathon in Vancouver. He staggered deliriously but courageously to the line, and then collapsed unconscious, not knowing until hours later that the line he had reached was still 200 meters from the finish.

23

TIME

TIME IS THE INTERNATIONAL language of the marathon. Before a race, on a street in Brazil, we met a group of Bolivian runners—mountain dwellers from an environment indescribably different from ours. We had only one shared word between the six of us: "marathon." Within seconds, we were all counting on fingers to exchange our best marathon times, pointing, shaking hands, laughing, and making faces of admiration. Those little numbers, utterly meaningless to anyone outside the world of marathons, are our badges, our insignia, our certificates of credibility, our global currency. That day, those numbers gave six strangers all we needed to know about one another and broke ground for the growth of friendship.

Time is not the only measure for the marathoner, but it is key. Times become targets and measures of accomplishment. Sub-5 hours, sub-4, sub-3, sub-2:30, sub-2:10, even (and it is already being talked about) sub-2 hours: each has a different resonance; each is coded with connotations of how much talent and training and effort it requires. Runners know exactly what each means, as our Bolivian friends did.

At elite levels, time is the vital, precise measure of effort. Only the unemotional clock, incapable of optimism or misjudgment, is a trustworthy guide to conserving resources for the final few miles. When the great Paula Radcliffe surged excitedly after the halfway point in her first marathon in 2002, it was time that cautioned her: "When I saw 5:06 for that mile I thought, 'Whoops, better slow it down.'" One or two seconds per mile gained or lost against the planned schedule can change the whole nature and outcome of the race. With the clock's help, runners become adept at planning and judging optimum pace, subdividing the seemingly meaningless marathon distance into precisely measured packages of effort.

All marathon runners are adept, too, at interpreting a kind of sliding scale that gives a time different meanings depending upon the gender, age, and experience of the runner. These days, a 2:25, for example, is a good but not wonderful time for a man of 25, but it's world-class for a man of 50 or for a woman. The system of "age grading" (a scale that translates times from older runners to the equivalent for those in their prime) creates a form of level playing field that is great fun for the older generation (and which can be disregarded by the younger).

The marathon's obsession with time can be wonderfully irrational. Even when Michel Bréal proposed the first marathon in 1894 in his letter to Pierre de Coubertin, he wondered what time the "Greek warrior" ran, so that "we could establish the record"—as though someone might have shown up in 490 BC with a stopwatch. No one can know how fast or how far the warrior ran, or even if he ran at all. The 26 miles, 385 yards, eventually settled on for the marathon provides none of the pleasing time/distance correlation of the 4-minute

Previous spread: The elite women at the ING New York City Marathon, including Paula Radcliffe, third from left, line up and start their own watches, despite a high-tech timer vehicle and accurate clocks at every mile.

Right: Modern time-keeping has made stopwatches, too heavy to carry far, a thing of the past.

26.2
EW YORK CITY MARATHON

"I live in Buffalo, and I was half-preparing even for snow in early Novembe
But the crowds make you want to work harder every mile. It makes it all th

734 Reichel, B, 54M 3:23:30
735 Gil Escamez, A, 45M 3:23:32
736 Eggerts, D, 35F 3:23:32
737 Kosakowski, M, 46M 3:23:33
738 Donoghue, K, 35M 3:23:34
739 Degrazia, M, 52F 3:23:34
740 Palau, R, 36M 3:23:34
741 Nishino, I, 43M 3:23:35
742 Varriano, M, 36M 3:23:35
743 Wahoff, M, 36M 3:23:36
744 Moore, J, 36M 3:23:37
745 Danzer, E, 40M 3:23:38
746 Moffatt, A, 35M 3:23:38
747 Coequyt, L, 60M 3:23:39
748 Nieto, J, 45M 3:23:40
749 Cradden, B, 61M 3:23:40
750 Mouthon, B, 37F 3:23:41
751 Kleber, M, 33M 3:23:41
752 Spagnolo, S, 25M 3:23:42
753 Karlsson, E, 38F 3:23:42
754 Carlier, D, 31M 3:23:42
755 Nasato, P, 41M 3:23:42
756 Botein, H, 38F 3:23:43
757 Lesimple, F, 31M 3:23:43
758 Fisher, K, 25F 3:23:44
759 Ogryzek, L, 24F 3:23:46
760 Brito, A, 48F 3:23:46
761 Negre, A, 37M 3:23:47
762 Westerberg, P, 30M 3:23:48
763 Castillo, G, 29M 3:23:49
764 Serrano, O, 30M 3:23:49
765 Rivas, J, 27M 3:23:49
766 Newell, E, 26M 3:23:50
767 Mitterer, F, 52M 3:23:50
768 Geukens, I, 38F 3:23:51
769 Auer, D, 23M 3:23:52
770 Gallacher, J, 26M 3:23:53
771 Gmelch, T, 27M 3:23:55
772 Hemberger, V, 46M 3:23:55
773 Stafford, J, 53M 3:23:55
774 Montingelli, S, 33M 3:23:56
775 Tyndall, M, 35M 3:23:56
776 Wong, R, 57M 3:23:57
777 Glas, F, 36M 3:23:57
778 Liberale, A, 35M 3:23:57
779 Hanewall, C, 29M 3:23:57
780 Kaltenbaugh, A, 38F 3:23:58
781 Midot, J, 43M 3:23:59
782 Basanti, E, 45M 3:24:00
783 Marshall, J, 33M 3:24:00
784 Hermanson, E, 37F 3:24:02
785 Skorpil, M, 49M 3:24:04
786 Kaicher, E, 28F 3:24:04
787 Curtidor, L, 39M 3:24:04
788 Schapendonk, R, 33M 3:24:05
789 Wells, M, 30M 3:24:05
790 Moore, R, 48M 3:24:05
791 Hamon, O, 40M 3:24:05
792 Huemer, P, 36M 3:24:05
793 Bernd, L, 34M 3:24:06
794 Kloc, Z, 47M 3:24:08
795 Dubbelman, D, 28M 3:24:08
796 Monroe, L, 36M 3:24:09
797 Helas, D, 50M 3:24:10
798 Christopher, B, 44M 3:24:11
799 Hidalgo, J, 37M 3:24:13
800 Bader, L, 22F 3:24:14
801 Blatt, J, 37M 3:24:14
802 Mentzer, J, 31M 3:24:15
803 Hansen, H, 48M 3:24:16
804 Lehrmann, M, 37M 3:24:17
805 Kuper, G, 28M 3:24:18
806 Triscott, J, 28M 3:24:18
807 Gunnarsson, P, 41M 3:24:18
808 Sussman, J, 26M 3:24:19
809 Samsel, J, 59M 3:24:20
810 Winfield, S, 41M 3:24:21
811 Reinecke, T, 48M 3:24:21
812 Naik, V, 28M 3:24:22
813 Fitzgerald, W, 40M 3:24:22
814 Repp, J, 32M 3:24:23
815 Joubert, F, 39M 3:24:24
816 Berg, J, 33M 3:24:25
817 Palacios, R, 45M 3:24:25
818 Bosmann, B, 53M 3:24:25
819 Quintanilla, M, 34M 3:24:25

2002 Harris, S, 34M 3:26:13
2003 Kammerer, R, 38M 3:26:13
2004 Corsini, J, 31M 3:26:13
2005 Kennedy, C, 39M 3:26:13
2006 Arnold, K, 39M 3:26:14
2007 Elstrom, P, 38M 3:26:14
2008 Meynard, L, 48M 3:26:15
2009 Wilson, D, 53M 3:26:17
2010 Anderson, S, 28M 3:26:17
2011 Manceau, C, 50M 3:26:18
2012 Howell, J, 25F 3:26:18
2013 Bizot, W, 37M 3:26:20
2014 Fischer, K, 40M 3:26:20
2015 Dow, D, 52M 3:26:21
2016 Keane, A, 31F 3:26:22
2017 Nodari, A, 56M 3:26:23
2018 Lee, M, 32M 3:26:23
2019 Thobor, R, 33M 3:26:23
2020 Murphy, M, 33F 3:26:25
2021 Vanelburg, H, 42F 3:26:25
2022 Hancox, I, 41M 3:26:25
2023 Thakran, D, 31M 3:26:26
2024 Esty-Kendall, J, 54M 3:26:26
2025 Quigley, J, 24M 3:26:27
2026 Mendoza, C, 27M 3:26:28
2027 Iacoviello, V, 38M 3:26:29
2028 Smid, W, 26M 3:26:29
2029 Louin, P, 40M 3:26:30
2030 Jonsson, L, 35M 3:26:31
2031 Moriber, P, 47M 3:26:31
2032 Peterson, N, 30M 3:26:31
2033 Font, D, 37M 3:26:32
2034 Gasparotto, L, 39M 3:26:33
2035 Midulla, P, 39M 3:26:34
2036 John-Alder, H, 50M 3:26:34
2037 Lopez, J, 34M 3:26:36
2038 Gravier, J, 33M 3:26:36
2039 Glick, T, 27M 3:26:36
2040 Zachara, M, 40M 3:26:39
2041 Jones, T, 33M 3:26:40
2042 Peace, J, 52M 3:26:40
2043 McCrohan, T, 31F 3:26:40
2044 Kinerk, L, 32M 3:26:40
2045 Barrett, D, 28M 3:26:42
2046 Stotter, W, 33M 3:26:42
2047 Tacconi, A, 28M 3:26:42
2048 Hable, F, 42M 3:26:42
2049 Moseley, C, 45M 3:26:43
2050 Perret, A, 33M 3:26:44
2051 Vasquez, M, 30M 3:26:44
2052 Breitbarth, M, 36M 3:26:45
2053 Brill, B, 26M 3:26:45
2054 Cummings, S, 24F 3:26:45
2055 Daub, D, 35M 3:26:46
2056 Cottet, F, 50M 3:26:46
2057 Sabesan, V, 26F 3:26:46
2058 Anthoine, P, 35M 3:26:47
2059 Fitzgerald, B, 23M 3:26:47
2060 Dunning, R, 47M 3:26:47
2061 Muratani, T, 21F 3:26:49
2062 Ealy, D, 27M 3:26:50
2063 Anderson, M, 30M 3:26:52
2064 Stafford, D, 28M 3:26:53
2065 Burnite, S, 36M 3:26:54
2066 Crager, J, 42M 3:26:54
2067 Berka, J, 51M 3:26:56
2068 Doscher, B, 26M 3:26:57
2069 Loredo, A, 36M 3:26:58
2070 Casey, E, 28F 3:26:59

3:27:00

2071 Van Meer, M, 24M 3:27:00
2072 Taft, D, 38M 3:27:01
2073 Bashforth, P, 30M 3:27:01
2074 Shen, A, 23F 3:27:01
2075 Conkling, T, 21M 3:27:02
2076 Joly, O, 27M 3:27:03
2077 Guenzi, C, 50M 3:27:03
2078 Wahle, H, 46M 3:27:03
2079 Fillon, J, 48M 3:27:04
2080 Killen, L, 40M 3:27:04
2081 Bayou, A, 26M 3:27:05
2082 Greenberg, A, 37M 3:27:05
2083 Tindill, T, 26M 3:27:06

2270 Flaherty, R, 39M 3:28:46
2271 Berfas, C, 28F 3:28:47
2272 Christensen, J, 41F 3:28:47
2273 Dunley, L, 41F 3:28:47
2274 Halasinski, M, 40M 3:28:48
2275 Reyes Vasquez, O, 36M 3:28:48
2276 Best, J, 43M 3:28:48
2277 Barrero, A, 54M 3:28:49
2278 May, G, 30M 3:28:50
2279 Smith, C, 49F 3:28:50
2280 Henson, J, 31M 3:28:50
2281 Keeney, C, 30M 3:28:51
2282 Singer, J, 22M 3:28:52
2283 Bordet, R, 30M 3:28:52
2284 Farias, D, 36F 3:28:52
2285 Torres, J, 26M 3:28:53
2286 De Santis, S, 48M 3:28:54
2287 Plankensteiner, W, 38M 3:28:54
2288 Fubel, J, 32M 3:28:54
2289 Andrews, D, 58M 3:28:55
2290 Perino, G, 49M 3:28:55
2291 Woller, M, 31M 3:28:55
2292 Estrup, C, 48M 3:28:55
2293 Cuahuizo, R, 20M 3:28:57
2294 Van Haperen, R, 51M 3:28:57
2295 Stephens, G, 41M 3:28:57
2296 Jara, D, 31M 3:28:57
2297 Algranti, A, 24M 3:28:58
2298 Ballereau, B, 46M 3:28:58
2299 Evans, T, 29F 3:28:58
2300 Lecointe, J, 42M 3:28:59
2301 Gordon, J, 33M 3:28:59
2302 Thomas, D, 41M 3:28:59
2303 Lehman, J, 43M 3:29:00
2304 Farley, C, 41M 3:29:00
2305 Agostini, M, 41M 3:29:00
2306 Vanderzyl, J, 39M 3:29:01
2307 Warren, A, 30M 3:29:01
2308 Isakov, J, 29M 3:29:01
2309 Hall, S, 44F 3:29:02
2310 Cascella, M, 41M 3:29:03
2311 Lopes, B, 33M 3:29:03
2312 Viso, J, 30M 3:29:04
2313 Marquez, T, 45M 3:29:04
2314 Muse, E, 25M 3:29:05
2315 Herbert, T, 39M 3:29:06
2316 Bernhardt, P, 60M 3:29:06
2317 Rabolini, P, 39F 3:29:07
2318 Cole, D, 42M 3:29:07
2319 Rocton, O, 38M 3:29:07
2320 Hill, J, 50M 3:29:08
2321 Redington, G, 37M 3:29:08
2322 Alvarez, J, 31M 3:29:08
2323 Smith, A, 41M 3:29:09
2324 Mackellar, S, 35M 3:29:09
2325 Joseph, B, 41M 3:29:10
2326 Levine, I, 43M 3:29:10
2327 Breen, B, 35M 3:29:11
2328 Bhambhani, A, 34M 3:29:11
2329 Nann, L, 23F 3:29:12
2330 Kottke, R, 37M 3:29:12
2331 Erme, J, 39M 3:29:12
2332 Byrne, W, 47M 3:29:13
2333 Kim, Y, 39M 3:29:14
2334 Hingstman, A, 46M 3:29:15
2335 Gualandi, V, 34F 3:29:17
2336 Schutz, R, 46M 3:29:17
2337 Casella, F, 32M 3:29:17
2338 Ichimura, N, 36M 3:29:18
2339 Gillon, S, 32F 3:29:19
2340 Harding, J, 45M 3:29:20
2341 Hoefen, K, 29F 3:29:20
2342 Brizard, P, 40M 3:29:21
2343 Miwa, S, 44M 3:29:21
2344 Flores, C, 36M 3:29:22
2345 Bugeaud, P, 42M 3:29:23
2346 Pueschel, C, 34M 3:29:23
2347 Sorrentino, F, 46M 3:29:24
2348 Buttenheim, E, 47M 3:29:24
2349 Martin, A, 35M 3:29:24
2350 Birkelo, J, 41M 3:29:25
2351 Vendryes, A, 35M 3:29:26
2352 Schuenemann, M, 40M 3:29:26
2353 Maloney, C, 66M 3:29:27
2354 Wilcox, R, 45M 3:29:27
2355 Conway, S, 27M 3:29:27

2539 Stuart, M, 44M 3:30:56
2540 Kruppa, C, 30F 3:30:56
2541 Westfall, C, 26F 3:30:57
2542 Viano, F, 29F 3:30:58
2543 Waguespack, J, 45M 3:30:58
2544 Sheridan, T, 47M 3:30:59
2545 Koninx, J, 51M 3:31:00
2546 Cascone, J, 24M 3:31:00
2547 Metzner, M, 30F 3:31:01
2548 Callahan, C, 22M 3:31:02
2549 Kelly, R, 31M 3:31:02
2550 Krainer, A, 39M 3:31:02
2551 Jekogian, M, 31M 3:31:03
2552 Clenin, B, 51M 3:31:03
2553 Henricksen, J, 28M 3:31:03
2554 Rice, G, 39M 3:31:04
2555 Cyrus, B, 32M 3:31:04
2556 Kaufmann, A, 23M 3:31:05
2557 Callow, J, 25M 3:31:05
2558 Talbot, S, 27M 3:31:05
2559 Braeuler, B, 52M 3:31:06
2560 Blanch, A, 35M 3:31:07
2561 Karvinen, E, 58M 3:31:07
2562 McAndrews, C, 42F 3:31:08
2563 Palumbo, R, 48M 3:31:10
2564 Jacobs, D, 53F 3:31:10
2565 Taylor, T, 25M 3:31:12
2566 Kramer, R, 35M 3:31:12
2567 Bogard, A, 33M 3:31:13
2568 Atri, R, 31F 3:31:13
2569 Hyams, C, 36M 3:31:15
2570 Gibbons, J, 31M 3:31:15
2571 Kiasumbwa, J, 35M 3:31:15
2572 Miller, J, 26F 3:31:17
2573 Deleo, F, 50M 3:31:17
2574 Gurr, S, 30M 3:31:17
2575 Clute, M, 24F 3:31:17
2576 Felter, H, 26F 3:31:17
2577 Harkin, P, 38F 3:31:18
2578 Alarcon, P, 34M 3:31:19
2579 Lukin, R, 35M 3:31:19
2580 Lalitte, J, 41M 3:31:20
2581 Lane, C, 44F 3:31:21
2582 Blakeslee, A, 25F 3:31:22
2583 Cordero, A, 43M 3:31:22
2584 Toth, M, 27M 3:31:23
2585 McGruther, J, 30F 3:31:23
2586 Gavanon, D, 48M 3:31:24
2587 Carpenter, M, 42M 3:31:24
2588 Dennihy, D, 49M 3:31:25
2589 Shah, S, 31F 3:31:26
2590 Buckwalter, A, 23F 3:31:26
2591 Chaffiotte, C, 38M 3:31:29
2592 Connors, E, 25F 3:31:30
2593 Thomas, D, 50M 3:31:30
2594 Kurak, D, 28M 3:31:31
2595 Chow, B, 25F 3:31:31
2596 Wiedemann, S, 33F 3:31:31
2597 Steinbrunner, J, 44M 3:31:32
2598 Capitani, A, 35M 3:31:32
2599 Petrilli, J, 42M 3:31:33
2600 Ricketson, P, 50M 3:31:35
2601 Geoghegan, P, 38M 3:31:35
2602 Mangan, J, 42M 3:31:36
2603 Turk, M, 36M 3:31:36
2604 Miller, M, 26F 3:31:37
2605 Russell, J, 35M 3:31:37
2606 Biancheri, M, 33M 3:31:38
2607 Biancheri, A, 35M 3:31:38
2608 Nevarez, J, 40M 3:31:38
2609 Kennedy, M, 54F 3:31:38
2610 Cox, C, 45M 3:31:39
2611 Kanter, J, 37M 3:31:40
2612 Jimenez, R, 28M 3:31:40
2613 Toomey, K, 32F 3:31:41
2614 Johnson, A, 37F 3:31:41
2615 Maes, P, 32M 3:31:41
2616 Ollivier, J, 41M 3:31:42
2617 Smith, B, 42F 3:31:43
2618 Oelkers, R, 28M 3:31:43
2619 Cardenas, M, 41M 3:31:45
2620 Black, J, 26M 3:31:45
2621 Stutz, T, 25F 3:31:46
2622 Danborg, P, 40M 3:31:46
2623 TronbsL, E, 38M 3:31:46
2624 Kopelson, H, 38F 3:31:46

2812 Marat, L, 55M 3:33:26
2813 Mathe, J, 48M 3:33:27
2814 Elberti, A, 26M 3:33:28
2815 Mayer, B, 31M 3:33:28
2816 Fornaro, E, 52M 3:33:28
2817 Hamilton, K, 26F 3:33:30
2818 Hughey, L, 26F 3:33:31
2819 Calo', A, 40M 3:33:32
2820 Fagala, R, 30M 3:33:33
2821 Epstein, K, 45M 3:33:34
2822 De Lorijn, L, 26F 3:33:35
2823 Verstraete, E, 42M 3:33:35
2824 Ceralli, P, 31M 3:33:36
2825 Stocker, E, 45F 3:33:36
2826 Leclercq, D, 27M 3:33:37
2827 Ermacora, P, 53M 3:33:37
2828 Canales, F, 45M 3:33:38
2829 Garagnani, E, 38F 3:33:39
2830 Baxendale, S, 38M 3:33:40
2831 Kriechhammer, B, 24M 3:33:40
2832 Buzeta, R, 48M 3:33:41
2833 De Bernardo, N, 49F 3:33:43
2834 Stanton, R, 37M 3:33:43
2835 Gelfand, G, 55M 3:33:43
2836 Godot, F, 43M 3:33:43
2837 Kavanagh, P, 45M 3:33:43
2838 Maffezzoli, M, 51M 3:33:45
2839 Capili, R, 30M 3:33:45
2840 Derrer, M, 25F 3:33:45
2841 Grace, P, 32M 3:33:46
2842 Toto, J, 31M 3:33:46
2843 Ayling, S, 28M 3:33:47
2844 Thomas, D, 29F 3:33:48
2845 Diaz Sabala, E, 34M 3:33:49
2846 Ramirez, S, 41M 3:33:49
2847 Dugan, J, 37M 3:33:50
2848 Young, B, 27M 3:33:50
2849 Birrer, R, 23M 3:33:52
2850 Niessing, D, 35M 3:33:53
2851 Furic, C, 48M 3:33:53
2852 Kristensen, J, 48M 3:33:54
2853 Marton, F, 30M 3:33:55
2854 Moran, W, 43M 3:33:57
2855 Ruiz, J, 40M 3:33:57
2856 Smith, R, 28M 3:33:58
2857 Cakebread, J, 49M 3:33:58
2858 Giannotti, M, 40F 3:33:58
2859 Bishop, M, 25M 3:33:59
2860 Geffraye, F, 34M 3:34:00
2861 Boesel, L, 50M 3:34:00
2862 Lowiner, A, 40M 3:34:00
2863 Cielusniak, D, 30M 3:34:01
2864 Fruscione, M, 32M 3:34:01
2865 Mayol-Bracero, E, 48M 3:34:02
2866 Priore, C, 34M 3:34:02
2867 Park, C, 45M 3:34:02
2868 Schmiemann, P, 43M 3:34:02
2869 Schaefer, J, 35M 3:34:03
2870 Morrow, J, 32F 3:34:03
2871 Lloyd, A, 38M 3:34:03
2872 McDonnell, C, 44M 3:34:03
2873 Stone, M, 52M 3:34:04
2874 Heller, R, 44M 3:34:04
2875 Smisek, D, 38M 3:34:05
2876 Kim, M, 41M 3:34:05
2877 Spielman, B, 36M 3:34:06
2878 Chambrin, H, 35M 3:34:06
2879 Maurer, R, 46M 3:34:06
2880 Verburg, G, 46F 3:34:07
2881 Cottone, E, 37F 3:34:07
2882 Thiriet, P, 43M 3:34:08
2883 Moratelli, A, 41M 3:34:09
2884 Lieck, N, 33M 3:34:09
2885 Rigby, A, 25M 3:34:10
2886 Chatman, K, 24F 3:34:10
2887 Foster, S, 30F 3:34:11
2888 Grossman, M, 47M 3:34:11
2889 Dr. Weihrauch, F, 48M 3:34:12
2890 Sawada, Y, 33M 3:34:12
2891 Dyke, A, 27M 3:34:12
2892 Riedl, M, 35M 3:34:12
2893 Hernandez, A, 26M 3:34:13
2894 Remy, E, 30F 3:34:13
2895 Draper, G, 39M 3:34:13
2896 Orsi, E, 35F 3:34:13
2897 Budde, P, 61M 3:34:13

3081 Power, A, 39M
3082 Randall, C, 52M
3083 Gardiner, P, 33M
3084 Calgaro, M, 29M
3085 Lovrek, M, 48M
3086 Geukers, J, 49M
3087 Shelton-Smith, K
3088 Lambert, S, 62F
3089 Sullivan, W, 47M
3090 Murray, S, 34M
3091 Shelley, T, 46M
3092 Olinto, S, 38F
3093 Saft, B, 30M
3094 Newman, J, 41M
3095 Maakheru, A, 43
3096 King, A, 34F
3097 Tran, T, 36M
3098 Kazukiewicz, R,
3099 Cottingham, K,
3100 Hewitson, H, 31
3101 Markowitz, L, 43
3102 Haindl, O, 37M
3103 Kane, M, 43M
3104 Turner, B, 46M
3105 Shelley, M, 26F
3106 Mella, J, 37M
3107 Hall, E, 32M
3108 Sandri, B, 39M
3109 Garino, C, 36M
3110 Mantari, J, 35M
3111 Mora, A, 27F
3112 Rosenthal, M, 40
3113 Raible, C, 30F
3114 Stahl, K, 41M
3115 Anthony, M, 44F
3116 Simon, J, 47M
3117 Norris, J, 45F
3118 Aigner, J, 44M
3119 Johnson, E, 26F
3120 Stopyak III, G, 32
3121 Hagenbucher, G,
3122 Becu, A, 37F
3123 Faruolo, T, 58M
3124 Brooks, P, 38M
3125 Freeman, J, 29F
3126 De Jong, C, 31M
3127 Nichols, D, 29M
3128 Benstead, A, 42F
3129 Fabel, D, 39M
3130 Rodriguez, R, 30
3131 Sepehrnia, M, 22
3132 Galgey, J, 31M
3133 Wegener, G, 44M
3134 Borges, J, 33M
3135 Fullem, J, 26M
3136 Dumont, E, 34M
3137 Sullenberger, L,
3138 Zagal, C, 32M
3139 Clarke, M, 45M
3140 Leterel, F, 30M
3141 Leclercq, A, 39M
3142 Bell, J, 31M
3143 O'Gorman, M, 45
3144 Rico, A, 56M
3145 Rigamonti, M, 31
3146 Vasquez Salazar,
3147 Aebersold, T, 43
3148 Ferrand, P, 40M
3149 Grob, P, 45M
3150 Dong, A, 47M
3151 Schmitz, K, 37F
3152 Fukuda, Y, 35M
3153 Angel, M, 35M
3154 Jewell, A, 25M
3155 Moyer, W, 49M
3156 Keane, W, 28M
3157 Mallo, L, 32M
3158 King, J, 38M
3159 Dodd, A, 30M
3160 Bardin, J, 51M
3161 Petrone, V, 39M
3162 Van Gaalen, B, 30
3163 McGrath, T, 44M
3164 Mathews, I, 33M
3165 Fennell, D, 34F
3166 Krasse, M, 32M

mile or the 10-second 100 meters. A pace of 5 or 6 or 10 minutes per mile divides beautifully into a 10- or 20-mile road race, but there is no tidy time pattern for the awkward, illogical marathon.

If it makes little sense to think in terms of time, why do almost all of us do it? If you dare, try telling runners that no finish times will be released after a marathon. Official times affirm the reality and worth of each runner's effort and, by recording it, make it seem permanent, a part of history. Runners love to have their name and time printed in the newspaper—watch them line up for souvenir copies the morning after the race. See them in the race, too, almost without exception, start and stop their own watches. They buy the paper not for information but for validation.

For a hundred years, race organizers struggled to find ways of recording an official time for every finisher. The answer was found in a Dutch farmyard. Wim Meijer had just been put in charge of the finish area for a 1993 race with 3,000 starters, and he anticipated chaos. The son of farmers, he knew that cows were tracked by radio frequency identification, through transponders in ear tags. He also thought of security key cards and their lightweight ID transponders. Meijer fitted 700 runners with a prototype chip, and in 1994 he launched his refined ChampionChip system.

Meijer's invention puts a tiny transponder into an individualized plastic chip laced to the running shoe. In combination with an energizing coil, and housed in a waterproof glass capsule, the transponder activates antennae implanted in rubberized mats on the roadway at the start, finish, and any number of points along the route. No longer do runners in big races fret about the time they lose in the crowds shuffling toward the start—their timing begins only when their chip crosses the mat. No longer do long lines clog the finish area while volunteers tear off tags—every time is instantly recorded, no matter how many scramble across the finish at once. No longer can cheats make their vainglorious entrance late in the race—mats at unannounced locations simply check for every runner. And no longer must family and friends wait for a breathless long-distance phone call to learn their runner's result—the chip program transmits progress instantly to the Internet. You can follow the real-time progress of a runner in Toronto from your computer in Tokyo.

The human mind needs to give purpose and value to the things it drives the body to do. We give value to travel by calling it a pilgrimage or a quest, or to war by fighting for a cause. The marathon is so demanding that we need to know it is intrinsically greater than merely three or four hours of unnecessary effort. Time affirms this greater meaning, measures its significance, and documents it as an accomplishment of permanent value. We can't all discover America or rescue Helen of Troy. But we can run a sub-2:30 marathon (or sub-4, or whatever your aspiration may be). Most of us will happily settle for that—and try next time to beat it.

Left: 30,000 names and finishing times from the previous day's ING New York City Marathon guarantee proud and happy runners, as well as a sold-out edition of the *New York Times*.

Left: The unobtrusive little ChampionChip, slotted on the shoelace.

Above: As each runner crosses the transponder mat, their times are recorded, while the clock shows their progress more conventionally.

24

OUT OF THE RIFT VALLEY

OF THE FASTEST 100 MARATHONS ever run, 58 were achieved by runners from the Rift Valley region of East Africa. To date, the once-impossible time of 2:07 has been beaten on 33 occasions—23 of those times by Ethiopian or Kenyan runners. Rift Valley runners have won 12 Olympic marathon medals in 12 games since 1960; they have won every men's Boston Marathon but one since 1988, every women's Boston but one since 1997, 7 of the last 8 men's races at New York, and 8 of the last 10 men's races at Berlin. The figures are extraordinary. The Germans and Italians are good at music, the Brazilians at soccer, the Swiss and the Sherpas at climbing mountains, but rarely have people from one small area so excelled in a globally popular activity.

"How can such relatively small and poor countries produce an endless supply of world class runners?" we asked Kenyan-born Lornah Kiplagat (now a Dutch citizen) before a race in New York.

"It's attitude and altitude, but there is part of your problem," she said, pointing to the passing traffic and a laden buffet table. "In Kenya we run for transportation and eat fresh food that we have usually grown ourselves. We live at altitude, we want to win, and we are very, very tough."

It's a good summary, but it leaves many questions. Why did this dominance happen so recently? Why is it only Kenyans and Ethiopians, and not people who live at even higher altitudes with lifestyles equally pure—the Peruvians, Bolivians, Nepalese? Is this supremacy impregnable? The best answers we can find lie in a mix of geography, adaptation, social history, and opportunity.

Standing on the edge of a high escarpment, you look out over a green plain that extends for 4,000 miles, from Ethiopia in the north, through Kenya and the eastern parts of Uganda and Tanzania. This is the Great Rift Valley. You feel the sun, but the air is cool and the climate perfect for year-round running, if you can cope with 8,000 feet of altitude.

We are in the Nandi Hills, near Eldoret, and from within 100 miles come 90 percent of the world-record-beating Kenyan runners. The red dirt roads are filled with people walking, herding cattle, or carrying produce, and children running barefoot, smiling and greeting you—"*Jambo!*" These kids run to school and back twice a day, some totaling 15 miles, which means 75-mile training weeks for 10 years by the time they are 17. They are lean, with the perfect teeth that indicate fresh sugar-free food.

Farther north, from within 100 miles of Bekoji on the rolling Ethiopian plateau come 90 percent of the world-record-beating Ethiopian runners. The soil is less red and the greetings are in a different language, but the climate is just as temperate and the people are just as lean and resilient, toughened from childhood on farms, where the work is done by hand, and from running. And the altitude is even higher here—10,500 feet.

Thousands of years ago, people spread from the north over the high but hospitable plains of

Previous spread: Tegla Loroupe trains near her home. Loroupe, Kenya's woman warrior, has run from humble origins in isolated rural West Pokot to become a champion and revered international leader.

Above: The high but hospitable plains of the Rift Valley are home to more than half of the world's best marathon runners.

what are now Ethiopia and Kenya. They were pastoralists as well as warriors. Many became cattle herders or cattle rustlers. Both required good running. Like that other great running culture, the Native Americans of the Southwest, they lived on a high plain with no horses and few rivers. Their transportation and communication infrastructure depended on their legs and lungs.

Adaptation over generations produced people fit for this altitude lifestyle of long running and rapid recovery. Much is still to be learned, but it is known that Rift Valley peoples are superlative in the transference of oxygen from the lungs into the bloodstream, a high count of oxygen-carrying blood cells, fast processing of lactic acid, and in their fine, light upper bodies and long leg muscles.

The Nepalese, another high-altitude people, share some but not all these characteristics. A recent study showed that their powerful climbers' thighs and backs make them the earth's "most efficient human haulers" of heavy weights. You climb the rugged Himalayas, but you run the rolling expanses of the Rift Valley.

An Ethiopian marathoner and a Kenyan track runner first revealed the power of Rift Valley running. Abebe Bikila was a palace guard when he won the Olympic marathon for Ethiopia in 1960 and 1964. And, from a few hundred miles south, Kip Keino became Kenya's hero when he beat the 1,500-meters world-record holder Jim Ryun in the high-altitude 1968 Mexico City Olympics.

Ethiopian sport, in the difficult decades since liberation from Italy in 1941, was centrally structured. Bikila and Mamo Wolde were soldiers. Today's best runners earn high incomes, and include great women such as Olympic champion and three-time Boston winner Fatuma Roba, London Marathon winner Derartu Tulu, and most recently Elfenesh Alemu. But Ethiopia's best have still not followed the Kenyans in moving in large numbers to Europe and America.

After Keino's success in 1968, the young Kenyans he inspired, English speaking and often well educated, were suddenly offered the opportunity of university education on American track scholarships. Keino, said to be Africa's second most admired man after Nelson Mandela, acted as mentor to many, who (mostly) returned to Kenya with valuable skills. But runners at home, including all women, still had to deal with tribal rivalries and a near-subsistence economy. For those good enough to make a national team, track and cross-country were the focus. The marathon, unfamiliar in a country with almost no paved roads, was not yet an option.

It was the advent of road-running prize money in the 1980s that suddenly turned a talent for distance running into an earning opportunity. Thousands of Kenyans have literally run to success, and the marathon has changed innumerable

Left: Ehtiopian Kutre Dulecha crosses the finish line, winning the Women's Amsterdam Marathon in 2005.

Kenyans' lives. Winners have gone home to build houses, buy farms and cattle, and provide education for their children and water systems for their villages.

Few lives were changed more than Tegla Loroupe's, and few have changed so many other lives for the better. Born into an isolated and traditionally inferior tribe, the West Pokot, Loroupe had to cajole her father into letting her attend school and permitting her to run. It was unseemly for a girl. At age 12, racing with a nail piercing her foot, she was second in the Kenyan cross-country trials. She was not selected, the first of several slights because, in tribal terms, she came from the "wrong side of the tracks." When European agents noticed her, she began to run road races abroad and persuaded the German coach Volker Wagner to guide her.

As she became internationally respected, the 4-foot-11, 86-pound sprite fearlessly began using her visibility to oppose the discrimination she had suffered. "When your country gives you no inspiration, you must be your own inspiration," she said.

In 1994, at New York City, Loroupe became the first African woman to win a major marathon. In West Pokot she was given two cows and 16 merino sheep, gifts more prestigious than her Mercedes-Benz race prize. When she won New York again in 1995, she was made a warrior, an honor never before conferred on a woman. Kenya's wealth of female talent began to claim the respect and

opportunity they had been denied through history.

Loroupe broke the world marathon record twice, but in her thirties her real story may be starting. She has created Peace Races to break down hatred, and established the Tegla Loroupe Peace Foundation to support children's rights and the campaign against AIDS. Traveling on a diplomatic passport, she has been invited to address the United Nations General Assembly. In Kenya people say, "Run like Tegla," just as Greeks call out, "Run like Louis."

Success in the marathon never comes easily, whatever your innate talent. The Rift Valley runners adopted the most demanding known training methods—the Ethiopians those from Sweden, and the Kenyans those from England's infamously rigorous cross-country tradition. They added their own group work, hard uphill intervals, long tempo runs, and sometimes three training sessions a day, all at high altitude. Few can match their arduous commitment.

Now the influence goes the other way. Elite runners around the world incorporate periods at altitude in their training. Many also adopt the training regimes of Kenya and Ethiopia. Increasing numbers go there to run and learn. It is a form of training pilgrimage, an act of homage to these extraordinary people and all they have achieved in the world of the marathon.

Above: "We live at altitude, we want to win, and we are very very tough," said Lornah Kiplagat. The lithe and mobile people of Kenya here compete at home, in their own Safaricom Marathon, inspired by British running legend Bruce Tulloh, who lived for some years in Kenya.

25

SOUVENIRS

"LIKE A PILGRIMAGE, the marathon makes me feel holy," said Philadelphia law professor Sally Gordon. "My medals prove I completed the journey. They represent some of the best days of my life." Indeed, these souvenirs are often almost sacred to their owners. Some, like pharaohs, ask in their wills to be buried in their most hallowed race T-shirt and running shoes, with the insignia that best prepare them for eternity—their marathon medals.

A casual poll revealed that most runners keep almost everything from a marathon, but not shorter races. "My medals hang on a special rack alongside my diploma and my wedding photos," said a runner from Dallas. "No question, these are my greatest accomplishments. I've put the medals in my will for my sister, who says she wants only these to inspire her always."

"I've made a big display of my medals," said another runner from Tampa. "When I have a tough day, I look at them and know that I can get through anything."

"I've put all my numbers and my medals in a scrapbook," said Joan Filipowski from Indiana. "When I'm old and gray, I want to show my grandchildren that you can do a task, no matter how big or impossible." A friend said it more succinctly: "I want my grandkids to have proof that I never just sat on my ass." These are people proud of earning renown comparable to the athletes of ancient Greece who were crowned in wreaths of olive or laurel.

Another friend's home was burgled recently. He was bereft. Not because he lost his laptop or his grandfather's shotgun, but because the thieves took his finisher's T-shirt from the inaugural Auckland, New Zealand, Marathon. He spent more time writing race organizers for a replacement than working on his insurance claim.

The inaugural Leading Ladies Marathon, in the unlikely location of Spearfish, South Dakota, had no cash sponsor and a limited budget, but director Elaine Doll-Dunn, a veteran of 108 marathons, nevertheless had beautiful finisher's medals designed. They were her single biggest expense. Queried about this extravagant souvenir, Elaine was aghast: "Heavens! The medal was the first thing I ordered. Each finisher is a winner. I'd go into personal debt before I'd cut that expense!"

Overcoming the marathon distance is like overcoming adversity in our lives. Finishing sets us apart. We beat the others who never started. We bettered the demons and an ordinary life. Every number, medal, T-shirt, space blanket, mug, necklace, and key chain reminds us that we are special, accomplished, and significant.

Previous spread: The marathoner's life is one of significant accomplishment, and many chart their careers by preserving souvenirs of each race. Selections in this chapter are from the collection of Les Potapczyk of Niagara Falls, Ontario.

Right: Even the shiny silver blankets distributed at marathon finish lines can remind the runner of those moments when they knew they had triumphed again over the challenge.

3026

2003 BOSTON MARATHON
BOSTON ATHLETIC ASSOCIATION

438

FORD
WNY AND No. PA FORD DEALERS

C MARATHON '91

NEW YORK CITY MARATHON
ING

NORWEST

CITGO
727

29692
PREMIER EVENT OF NEW YORK ROAD RUNNERS
Les J Potapczyk, M50
CAN
2003
BUS

1455

Sh
8

MARATHON '92

RD BUFFALO MARATHON '9

29th MARINE CORPS MARATHON™

LOS AN
MARAT

JANUARY 11

1623

17005

CITGO
CIT

455

IRISH
FirstCommand
NO FEDERAL OR MARINE CORPS ENDORSEMENT IS IMPLIED

56

CORRAL A

FORD

Buffalo Marathon '9

BOSTON M

3734

570

The Human Race

A631

POTAPCZYK, Les J, 50 CAN

MANU
HANC

00TH BOSTON
MARATHON®
VCO
653

CHEMICAL
Les Potapczyk
Canada
3:16:07

5975

Europa wird eins.
EUROPA '92
BERLIN

Shell

NYC MARATHON '9

Previous spread: "Each finisher is a winner," said one race director, speaking for all. Finishers' medals are the ultimate testimony to achievement, and are valued as much as Olympic winners' medals.

Left: For marathon runners, collectibles are not things you acquire or buy, but what you earn. For race numbers to have value, they must first be exposed to 26.2 miles of weather, road dust, sweat, and sometimes tears.

Above: "Never underestimate the power of a T-shirt," said New York's Fred Lebow. The race T-shirt, unknown before the 1970s, has become a kind of coveted insignia, a heraldic symbol of accomplishment, a travel memento, and a new art form.

26

HEROES 1982–2003

Alberto Salazar **United States (born Cuba),** b. 1958
Best time: 2:08:13 (1981)
His three sensational wins at New York and one at Boston made the marathon a global TV phenomenon. Seeming to absorb unlimited pain, he ran the fastest debut, broke the world record, and won legendary duels against Rodolfo Gomez and Dick Beardsley.

Grete Waitz **Norway, b. 1953**
Best time: 2:24:54 (1986)
She single-handedly transformed the women's marathon. She broke the world record four times (2:34:48 to 2:25:29), was the first world champion (1983), second at the Olympics (1984), and won New York nine times. The former teacher was a track and cross-country star before being lured to the marathon.

Rosa Mota **Portugal, b. 1958**
Best time: 2:23:29 (1985)
She zestfully won the first true championship for women, the 1982 European, and did much for women's acceptance as marathon equals. She won the European championship twice more, the world championship, world cup, Boston, Chicago, London, Osaka, Tokyo, and the 1988 Olympics.

Rob de Castella **Australia, b. 1957**
Best time: 2:07:51 (1986)
World-record breaker, world champion (1983), twice Commonwealth champion and Boston record breaker, he combined physical power with astutely varied tactics. Won from the front (Boston 1986), from well behind (Brisbane 1982), and with a blazing last mile (Rotterdam 1983).

Toshihiko Seko **Japan, b. 1956**
Best time: 2:08:38 (1983)
Seko led Japan back to the top ranks of the world marathon, winning in Boston (twice), London, Chicago, and four times in Fukuoka (equaling Frank Shorter's record). He combined the meticulous planning of his revered *"sansei"* coach, Kiyoshi Nakamura, with his own fervor: "You must run on the edge of death."

Carlos Lopes **Portugal, b. 1947**
Best time: 2:07:12 (1985)
Insidious acceleration gave him Olympic victory in 1984, at 37 the oldest champion. At 38, he broke the world record. From humble origins, he was the Olympic 10,000-meter silver medalist and twice world cross-country champion, running, it was said, "with the naturalness of a countryman scything corn."

Joan Benoit United States, b. 1957
Best time: 2:21:21 (1985)

The image of her running out of the tunnel into the sunlit acclaim of the Los Angeles Coliseum in 1984 is an indelible icon of women's emergence, winning their first Olympics with a spirited power worthy of the marathon's rich history. She won nine major marathons, and broke Waitz's world record.

Ingrid Kristiansen Norway, b. 1956
Best time: 2:21:06 (1985)

Her 1985 world record lasted 13 years, supplanting Waitz and Benoit. She won Chicago, New York, Boston twice, and London four times, helping to make it a world-class event. She broke world track records (5,000 and 10,000 meters), and was world cross-country champion.

Steve Jones Wales (represented Great Britain), b. 1955
Best time: 2:07:13 (1985)

From rigorous origins in industrial Wales and British cross-country, he ran the 1984 Olympic 10,000 meters. He then took off in the marathon, with a world record at Chicago in 1984. He won London, Chicago again just off the new world mark, and the 1988 New York.

Priscilla Welch England, b. 1944
Best time: 2:26:51 (1987)

Standards for older women were transformed when she blazed into action at 37. Sixth at the 1984 Olympics at 39, she moved to altitude in the United States with her husband-coach, and at 42 set her long-standing masters world record at London and won New York outright. Breast cancer slowed but did not stop her.

Douglas Wakiihuri Kenya, b. 1963
Best time: 2:09:03 (1989)

The first of the great Kenyans trained in Japan under Nakamura, and ran with an impassive Asian serenity. He won the 1987 world championship, took silver in the 1988 Olympics, and won the Commonwealth Games and world cup, as well as London and New York. He is a composer and singer, in Kenyan and Japanese.

Ibrahim Hussein Kenya, b. 1958
Best time: 2:08:14 (1992)

Hussein, with Wakiihuri, brought Kenya to the front of the marathon world, winning New York, Honolulu three times, and Boston twice, including his unforgettable 1988 win by one second over Juma Ikangaa. A University of New Mexico graduate in economics, he became a sports administrator in Kenya.

Gelindo Bordin Italy, b. 1959
Best time: 2:08:19 (1990)

His bearded face carved deep in suffering reminded one commentator of Jesus carrying the cross, as he fought to win the 1988 Olympic gold. He won eight major marathons, including the European championship twice, took a world championship bronze, and became the only male Olympic champion to win Boston.

Katrin Dorre-Heinig East Germany (Germany after 1990), b. 1961
Best time: 2:24:35 (1999)

The most consistently successful marathoner, she ran sub-2:30 21 times, 1982-2000, winning 24 major races. After Olympic and world bronze medals (1988, 1991), and world cup wins, London twice, Tokyo three times, and Osaka four times, her fastest time was at 38.

John Campbell New Zealand b. 1949
Best time: 2:11:04 (1990)

Rewrote the over-40 world records, highlighted by his Boston 2:11:04. He placed 12th in the 1988 Olympics, and set masters marks at Los Angeles, Boston and New York. "He'd run right through a garbage truck," said one New Yorker, as the former offshore fisherman scowled and strove to fifth overall there.

Tegla Loroupe Kenya, b. 1973
Best time: 2:20:43 (1999)

As the first African woman to win a major marathon (New York 1994, 1995) she achieved something of social as well as sporting significance. She broke the 13-year-old world record, broke it again, won in London, Berlin and Rotterdam, and is still a pioneer, heading the Tegla Loroupe Peace Foundation.

Fatuma Roba Ethiopia, b. 1973
Best time: 2:23:21 (1998)

The first African woman to win the Olympic marathon grew up on a humble, high-altitude farm and was almost unknown until she flowed with seeming ease to that epoch-making 2-minute victory in 1996. Outdoing even her great Ethiopian precursor Abebe Bikila, she went on to win Boston three times.

Gezahegne Abera Ethiopia, b. 1978
Best time: 2:07:54 (1999)

The first man to win Olympic and world championship gold (2000, 2001) used the same masterly tactics to win Fukuoka (three times) and London (2003). His 2003 wedding to Elfenesh Alemu (fourth, Olympic marathon 2004) was in Addis Ababa Stadium with 25,000 guests and a 600-foot bridal train.

Naoko Takahashi Japan, b. 1972
Best time: 2:19:46 (2001)

The first native Japanese to win an Olympic marathon (2000); a year later she became the first woman to break 2:20. That double gave her canonical status in marathon-worshiping Japan, where a weekly comic book celebrates her achievements as "Daughter of the Wind."

Catherine Ndereba Kenya, b. 1972
Best time: 2:18:47 (2001)

World champion (2003), world-record breaker, Olympic silver medallist (2004), four-time Boston and three-time Chicago winner, she is arguably the greatest even of the Kenyans. Showed remarkable recovery when she won the 2001 Avon Global 10K only seven days after her world record marathon.

Khalid Khannouchi Morocco (moved to United States 1993, citizen 2000), b. 1971
Best time: 2:05:38 (2002)

After breaking the world record as a Moroccan, the first man under 2:06, he broke it again as an American, the first man since Clayton to do that double. He still has three of history's fastest seven marathons, with three wins at Chicago and one at London.

Ed Whitlock Canada (born England), b. 1931
Best time (for age): 2:54:49 (2004)

A retired engineer in his seventies is an unexpected marathon hero, but his 2:54:49 at age 73 is perhaps the greatest performance for age in marathon history. He has compiled groundbreaking performances since rediscovering his love of running in his late forties.

Paul Tergat Kenya, b. 1969
Best time: 2:04:55 (2003)

The great Kenyan has won only one marathon, but did it in a world record, the first man under 2:05. Invincible in the world cross-country (five successive wins) in the 1990s, and brilliant at half-marathon, he kept running fast seconds and thirds in marathons, until Berlin 2003 proved his heroic quality.

Paula Radcliffe England, b. 1973
Best time: 2:15:25 (2003)

Three minutes faster than any other woman, owning four of history's best five performances, she has twice broken the world record, and has won London, Chicago, New York, and the 2005 World Championship—every marathon she has entered, except one injury-afflicted Olympic dropout.

26.2

THE ECSTASY

IT IS THE FINISH that gives meaning to the marathon. The finish is not merely the end of a long and arduous journey, years of preparation and hours of courageous effort, it is the completion of that journey, its destination and purpose. The final step of the race is the summit of the mountain. It is the moment when the message is delivered. Without reaching the finish line, the marathon is just another long run.

For the runner, the last 365 yards are often a near-delirium state of confused external images and sounds, physical sensations, and inward emotions. All around (for most runners) are the half-seen, half-real figures of other finishers, their faces and bodies showing the full gamut of reactions. Some raise their arms in triumph and some shuffle in pain; some glow and some cry. Beyond them on the sidelines are blurred spectators and the sketchy features of this final phase of the course—the target of so much hopeful traveling. The first sight of the Finish banner lifts every runner's spirits—they will all recall that moment years later.

The final approach is often a tunnel of sound, with the crescendo of the crowd's cheers, pulsating music, and the voice of the public address announcer growing louder. Mingling with this external noise are the insistent calls from the runner's body. Tiredness and pain are demanding that the whole thing stop, yet overriding these calls are the stronger, swirling emotions of relief, delight, and pride of accomplishment.

Some think, "Rejoice, we conquer!" Some recall the many great runners who have gone before down those final 385 yards. Some reflect on the whole rich history of this unique sport. Some mentally add this marathon to their collection. Some repeat, "I did it, I did it!" Others share the moment, finishing hand-in-hand with a family member or partner. (One we know suddenly knelt in front of his girlfriend five yards from the finish and proposed. They're now married.) Some run in alongside a friend—sometimes one of those "instant" but genuine friends discovered when runners support each other along a marathon course. Some think of the person or cause that they dedicated their race to. Ultimately, it is finishing that makes the run worthy of the cause.

The rewards for finishing seem to vary widely. The race winners can earn prize money, sponsorships, instant celebrity, and lasting fame, while those further back get a medal with no commercial

Previous spread: The dedicated Emil Zatopek inspired a generation of runners. His training innovations included sometimes carrying his wife Dana, an Olympic javelin champion, on his back. Here they celebrate another gold medal, a joyous victory earned by rigorous training.

Right: Wrapped in joy, Jose Javier Conde of Spain privately meditates on his victory in the men's T46 Marathon at the Sydney 2000 Paralympic Games.

value and a crumpled Mylar blanket. The differ-
ence is only apparent. In reality, a world-record
winner receives exactly the same reward as every
finisher—the satisfying sense of having succeeded
against the odds, the knowledge of having proved
inner strength, and the closure of having completed
a quest. The individual nature of running makes
the fulfillment it gives profoundly personal. The
great thing about gaining self-esteem from finishing a marathon is that every runner knows it's not
just vanity or self-importance—they really did it,
the hard way, and they have the medal to prove it.

In truth, a marathon has no finish. Its effects
are carried for life within the body, the memory,
the life story, and the self-image. The marathon's
long, inspiring history and its cultural importance
in the modern world add another dimension, a
deeper significance. Finishing a marathon is a contribution to something that is more like a
movement than a sport. To finish a marathon is to
attain a small piece of immortality.

Left: To finish a marathon is to find a moment of joy,
relief, introspection, or prayer—perhaps all four at
once. Emotions at the finish line are various and visible.

Above: An overcome runner receives her finisher's medal.

Right: "I did it!" The loneliness of the long-distance runner soon ends in this age of post-race cell phone calls to friends and family, as witnessed at the Flora London Marathon.

Following spread: Jubilation at the finish.

INDEX

SOURCES

The following is a select list of sources that were extremely helpful in the writing of *26.2: Marathon Stories*

BOOKS

Rich Benyo and Joe Henderson, *Running Encyclopedia*

Walter Bortz II, MD, *Dare to be 100*

Jane Brody, *The New York Times Book of Health*

John Bryant, *The London Marathon*

Pamela Cooper, *The American Marathon*

Tom Derderian, *Boston Marathon. The History of the World's Premier Running Event*

Jean Driscoll, *Determined to Win, the Overcoming Spirit of Jean Driscoll*

Jon Entine, *Taboo! Why Black Athletes Dominate Sports*

Norman Giller, *Marathon Kings*

Roger Gynn, *The Guinness Book of the Marathon*

Rob Hadgraft, *The Little Wonder: Alfred Shrubb, World Champion Runner*

Bernd Heinrich, *Why We Run: A Natural History*

Hal Higdon, *Boston. A Century of Running*

International Olympic Committee: Official Reports (especially 1896, 1908)

Steve King and Dan Cumming, *Running in the Zone*

Charles Lyons (editor), *The Quotable Marathoner*

David E. Martin, PhD and Roger W.H. Gynn, *The Marathon Footrace*, and *The Olympic Marathon*

Tom McNab, Peter Lovesey and Andrew Huxtable, *An Athletics Compendium: An Annotated Guide to the U.K. Literature of Track and Field*

Trisha Meili, *I Am the Central Park Jogger*

Peter Nabokov, *Indian Running*

Olympic Museum, Lausanne, Switzerland: *The Olympics. Athens to Athens, 1896-2004*

Peter Pfitzinger and Scott Douglas, *Advanced Marathoning*

Roger Robinson, *Running in Literature*

Bill Rodgers and Scott Douglas, *The Idiot's Guide to Running*

Edward S. Sears, *Running Through the Ages*

Jock Semple, John J. Kelley and Tom Murphy, *Just Call Me Jock*

Alfred Shrubb, *Running and Cross Country Running*

John Stevens, *The Marathon Monks of Mount Hiei*

James E. Sullivan, *Marathon Running*

Dick Traum, *Victory for Humanity*

Sandy Treadwell, *The World of Marathons*

Joan Ullyot, *Women's Running*

Mel Watman, *Encyclopedia of Athletics* (3 editions)

Mark Will-Weber (editor), *The Quotable Runner*

JOURNALS

AIMS (Association of International Marathons) Monthly Newsletter

Athletics Weekly

Marathon and Beyond

New York Runner

New York Times

New Zealand Runner

Race Results Weekly

Runner's World

Running Stats

Running Times

The Washington Post

Article, "What Did Women Wear to Run?" by Ann Buermann Wass and Clarita Anderson, published in DRESS, Volume 17, 1990

Article, "Two Finish Lines" by Ron Rubin, PhD, published in The Jewish Journal of Los Angeles, March 25, 2005

WEBSITES

CoolRunning.com

ChampionChip.com

Fifty Plus Fitness Organization, www.50plus.org

International Olympic Committee

**THE AUTHORS WOULD LIKE TO ACKNOWLEDGE THE
FOLLOWING PEOPLE WHO AGREED TO BE INTERVIEWED**

Deborah Armstrong; I.W.Barkis, PhD; David Barrington; Jonathan Beverly; Marc Chalufour; Tim Chamberlain; Dave Cundy; Elaine Doll-Dunn; Patrick Doyle and Susan Knights; Jean Driscoll; Julia Emmons; Jack Fleming; Bill Frecklington; John Hanc; Nobby Hashizume; Barbara Huebner; Kate Q. Ince; Ross Jackson; Annemarie Jutel; Lornah Kiplagat; Pieter Langerhorst; Tegla Loroupe; (The late) Arthur Lydiard; David Martin, PhD; Bertha McGruder; Linda McKeldin; Elana Meyer; Lorraine Moller; David Monti; Phil Olsman; Bill Orr; Les Potapczyk; Gloria Ratti; Larry Rawson; Antoni Reavis; Ian Ridpath; Anne Roberts; Federico Rosa; Ron Rubin, PhD; Kaye Durland Spilker; Allan Steinfeld; Al Storie; Brian Taylor; Cathy Troisi; Bruce Tulloh; Greg Vitiello; Volker Wagner; Richard Willis; Kris and Joe Wirth.

MARATHONS VISITED

Asian Games; Avon (Atlanta, Waldniel, San Francisco, Ottawa, Los Angeles, Paris); Boston; Canberra; Christchurch; City of Los Angeles; Commonwealth Games; Fiji; Flora London; Goodwill Games; Grandma's; Honolulu; ING New York City; ING Ottawa; Lake Kawaguchi; LaSalle Bank Chicago; Leading Ladies; Manila; Manukau City; Marine Corps; More; Napa Valley; Niagara Fallsview Casino Resort International; Olympic Games; Pittsburgh; real-Berlin; Rotorua; Royal Victoria; Stamford; Twin Cities; Vancouver; Vermont City; Walt Disney World; Wellington City; Wiri, Manukau City; World Championships; World Cup; World Masters Championships.

PICTURE CREDITS

ACKNOWLEDGMENTS

Angel Editions and Madison Press Books offer special thanks to Julaine Brent, Les Potapczyk and Al Storie (www.alfieshrubb.ca) for allowing us to borrow and photograph their precious marathon souvenirs. Thanks to Micah Toub for his invaluable help with the initial research and conceptualization of the book. Thanks also to "The Body in Question" model Zoë McPhee, to Greig Dymond for his careful read of the text, and to Edward Pond for original photography.

For their assistance and generosity with their amazing photographs, thanks to: Amateur Athletic Foundation of Los Angeles; Charles Jay Bawcom; Pat Bigold/Honolulu Marathon; Jim Boka/Antarctica Marathon; Boston Athletic Association; Boston Public Library; Mike Bowen; James Bunton/Canada Sports Hall of Fame; Bill Burleigh/Big Sur International Marathon; Cliff Crase, Brenda Martin/*Sports 'n' Spokes* magazine; Richard Donovan/North Pole Marathon; Jean Driscoll; Mattia Durli/Sahara Marathon; Diane Ellis/Reggae Marathon; Robert Festino; Graeme Hannon/Blackmores Sydney Marathon; Tim Jackson, Patrice Malloy/Safaricom; Inge Johnson; Jungfrau Marathon; Leo Kulinski; Enrico Lodi/Maratona d'Italia Memorial Enzo Ferrari; Graham Maitland/Ryde Harriers; Marathon Popular de Valencia; Maratona della Citta di Roma; Brian Masck, Steve Jessmore/*Flint* journal; New York Road Runners; Stanislav Nikuli/Siberian Ice Marathon; Mariusz Peczek; Mark Peterson/Redux; Anouk Rouffieux; Victah Sailer/Photo Run; Carlos Salguero Solugraf/Coban Half Marathon; Scotiabank Toronto Waterfront Marathon; David Scranage; Dr. Ernst and Wiepke van Aaken; Dirk Jan van de Pol/ChampionChip; Wellesley College Archives.

An Angel Edition for Madison Press Books

Editorial direction and art direction Sara Angel
Project Editor Amy Hick
Book Design Alicia Kowalewski
Design assistance and production Luke Despatie
Photo research and permissions Bao-Nghi Nhan
Substantive Editor Laurie Coulter
Copy Editors Barbara Czarnecki and Anna Filippone
Proof reader and Indexer Patricia Holtz

Madison Press Books

Editorial Director Wanda Nowakowska
Vice President, Business Affairs and Production Susan Barrable
Production Manager Sandra L. Hall